FOREVERNESS:

The Collected Poems of Jean Barlow Hudson

Books by Jean Barlow Hudson:

Poetry

Foreverness: The Collected Poems of Jean Barlow Hudson
(Fallen Timbers Press, 1993)

Fiction

Rivers of Time
(Avon Press, 1979)

Foreverness

The Collected Poems of
Jean Barlow Hudson
Edited by Rex A. Hudson

FOREVERNESS

First Fallen Timbers Printing — November 1993.

Library of Congress Catalog Card Number 93-73434

ISBN 0-9638741-0-1

Front cover and title-page photo: Old Rag Mountain, Shenandoah National Park, Virginia, by Rex A. Hudson

Jacket and title-page design: Vie Design Studios, Inc.
Typesetting: Beljan, Ltd.
Printing: Thomson-Shore, Inc.

Publisher: Fallen Timbers Press
P.O. Box 710
Yellow Springs, Ohio 45387

For Jean

CONTENTS

Introduction   xv

Prologue   1

I
On Poetry

On Poetry	5
The Poetry of Living	6
An Unheeded Craft	7

II
Childhood

Carnival Boy	11
Calliope	12
Puppet	13
Deserted	14
Make-Believe	14
Dawn Kiss	15
Little Mother	16
A Poem for Vesta	17
Stillwater Creek	18

III
College

Lyric to June	21
Desolation	22

Lyric to Life   23
Star Folk I   24
Star Folk II   25
Love in the Springtime   26
Entreaty in Autumn   27
Leafless Tree   27
Study Hour   28
Lament of a Sculptor's Model   29
Litany   30

IV

Springtime in Wartime

The Approaching Calamity   35
Specter of Spring   37
Morning Sky   38
Beneath the Birches   39
Bereft of Poetry   40
To a Brother on the Frontline   41
Wild Bird   43
Seagulls over an Inland Field   44
Warning to a World at War   45
The World's Future   46

V

Love

Eternal Love   49
Transcontinental   51
Oleander Bush   53
Seedless Ecstasy   53
Woman at the Window   54
The Watcher   55
Meeting   56
Desertion   56
Primary Palette   57
The Savage   58
Quiet Love   59

VI

The Heart

Heart of the Matter	63
A Done Deed	64
Death of Mohandas Gandhi	65

VII

Wyoming

Wind River Canyon	69
Wyoming Legend	70
Hidden Beauty	76
Beneath the Aspens	77

VIII

Foreign Places

On the Beach at Al Khobar	81
Desert Winds	82
Street Scene in Amman	83
Afternoon in Lahore	84
Rainy Season in Manila	85
Hunt on the Gambia	86
Famine	87
Prayer Beads	88

IX

Identity

Identity	93
Phantasy of the Passing Train	94
Sounds of Bells and Trains	95
None Are Alone	96
Jungle	97
Standing Alone	98
Mask-Making Workshop	99
The Elements of Verbal Subjugation	100
Driving Through Mist	101
Disconnected	102
Moribund Spirit	103

X

Family

The Messenger	107
Epiphany to my Son	108
A Little Boy at Evening	109
Little Stranger	109
Cider-Making	110
A Mother's Pain	111
Housekeeping	112
Absence	112
Blood Bond	113
Chariots of Fire	114
Conflict at Home	115
A Daughter's Departure	116

XI

Summer

A Straight Road to Plain City	119
Stubborn in Summer	119
Summer Storm	120
Peeping Tom	121
Noise Pollution	123
Repose of the Night	124

XII

Garden

Separation	127
Garden Vine	128
Trace Elements	129
As the Stalk Withered	130

XIII

Friendship

Rain	133
Unbroken Filly	134
Mislaid Jewel	135
Sisterhood	136
Airwaves of Memory	137

Driven Woman   138
Dinner Party   139

XIV
Protest

Ideal World   143
The Birthright Custodians   144
First Strike   145
Soft Targets   146
The Data Collector   147
Ululating   148

XV
Autumn

Season of the Poets   153
Autumn Sonata   154
Old October   155
Season's End   156
October Woman   157
November Forenoon   157
Weeping Forest   158
Wind in Autumn   158

XVI
Nocturnes

November Night   161
Waiting Alone at Night   162
Nocturnal Meeting   162
Night Walk   163
Song of the Night   164

XVII
Time

Corridors of Time   169
Entropy of Me   170
Chords of Fate   171
Rainy Day   172
Inner and Outer Time   172
Our Moment in Time   173

XVIII
Winter

The Coldest Winter	177
Frosty Night	178
Etching	178
Illusion in Winter	179
Infants of Destiny	180
Dream of the Winter Solstice	181

INTRODUCTION

O NE DAY when I was ten, I learned to appreciate my mother Jean's poetic creativity and realized just how little of it I had. It was 1957 and, as usual, a pleasant sunny day in Cochabamba, Bolivia. She and I were sitting on the patio of our bungalow; I was struggling with an English-class assignment for the American Calvert School, and she was reading and writing and enjoying the fragrant, exotic mix of trees, plants, and flowers in the large garden, enclosed by a thick, eight-foot-high, adobe-brick wall. In response to my plea for help with the exercise, Jean explained (I always called her by her first name) something about the elements of composing a verse of poetry. She then asked me to see if I could compose a few lines, and she went inside the house to give the day's instructions in Spanish to the maid and the cook (one of the advantages of living in a developing country) and to do some typing on a novel. About an hour later, my paper was still blank, and I was completely stumped. Not wishing to disappoint my mother with the realization that I was totally lacking in creativity, I pulled out a large volume of poetry from the bottom of a pile of books, furtively cribbed what I recall were a couple lines (possibly four at the most) from the middle of a poem selected at random, and reburied the book.

Shortly thereafter, her rapid-fire typing stopped, and she came back outside and asked how I was coming along. I showed her the copied verse, and she acted impressed that I had composed such a well-crafted couplet. Then, noting reflectively how it reminded her of a certain poem, she pulled out the same book and, to my amazement and great discomfort, flipped to the very poem from which I had extracted the lines and began reading it aloud, by which time I had slumped practically under the glass table, too ashamed to look at her. She was not angry when she slapped the covers of the book closed with stern finality, only disappointed. Apparently resigned to my lack of creativity, she sighed and then resumed helping me compose a few lines that rhymed, although I contributed very little. It was a humiliating lesson in the writing of poetry and about as far as I ever got in that endeavour.

In retrospect, the whole embarrassing incident could have been avoided had I listened more closely to her fundamental rule of poetry — that anyone contemplating composing a poem should first have an idea, or what she has described in "On Poetry" as the "tendril of thought" on which a poem is predicated. (It probably would also have helped if I had been old enough to have some poetic ideas.) Someone as creative as Jean could get an idea for a poem by simply watching the hummingbirds in the garden darting in and out and the butterflies fluttering about or "pausing on the garden vine to brush their wings," as she describes it in "Garden Vine."

Jean's poetic sensibility was shaped by the school of established poets that included the likes of Conrad Aiken, W.H. Auden, T.S. Eliot (perhaps reflected in "Transcontinental" by the phrase "they come and go"), Robert Frost, Robinson Jeffers, Edgar Lee Masters, and Carl Sandburg. More contemporary poets who had an influence on her included two authors of books on writing poetry — John Ciardi and Judson Jerome (the latter was a friend of hers). Whether describing birds, trees, places, people, or time itself, her poems tend to be centered on a specific thought, emotion, person, place, et cetera, as opposed to the often cryptic ramblings of the many self-obsessed and confessional poets who use poetry as a therapeutic medium, in the tradition of Ann Sexton and Sylvia Plath, for example. I cannot offer any valid technical comparison, however, not being familiar enough with the work of Sexton and Plath or other feminist poets. In any case, it may not be fair or valid to compare Jean with professional women poets who wrote or write poetry full-time and had it published regularly.

Although the 130 poems in this volume constitute Jean's only book of poetry, her relatively small output of poems was still respectable for someone who found time to write poetry only occasionally, after she became a mother of three sons and subsequently lived in a series of foreign countries. Moreover, once free of her sons she gave birth to a daughter at age fifty and started motherhood all over again. She also devoted much of her creative energy to writing novels, one of which, *Rivers of Time*, was published in 1979.

For some professional poets, such as Mona Van Duyn, far too many occasional writers of poems now consider themselves poets. She has a point. If 40 million Americans claim in a Roper Poll that they write poetry, that does not necessarily mean the United States has 40 million poets. As the departing Poet Laureate Consultant in Poetry for the Library of Congress, Van Duyn also noted in a lecture in May 1993 that the term "poet" used to be reserved for professional poets like herself, those who write and publish poetry regularly. She questioned whether someone who has published only a single volume of poetry can be considered a poet. By that somewhat restrictive definition, however, Vincent Van Gogh, who was able to sell only one painting in his brief lifetime, was not a real painter.

It would seem that a more important criterion than the number of books of poetry a poet has published should be simply whether he or she is a good poet or a mediocre poet (and Van Duyn is a well-known judge in that regard). The vast majority of people who consider themselves poets, and many of those who have published poems, no doubt fit into the mediocre category. Clearly, the quantity of volumes of poetry published by a poet or sold by a publisher is not a reliable indicator of the quality of the poetry. According to Van Duyn, publishers print fewer than 500 copies of the poetry books of even the best poets. And hardly any serious poet would associate the 'poetry' of Rod McKuan, whose volumes sold hundreds of thousands of copies in the 1970s and 1980s, with quality poetry.

With a B.A. degree in literature and the poems in this volume of exquisite, memorable poetry to her credit, Jean was certainly qualified to call herself a poet, even if she was known only locally for her poetry. She considered herself to be a poet, and she wrote poems of exceptional resonance and depth. For Jean, the act of composing a poem was a cathartic end in itself. Once she expressed her thoughts or emotions in a poem, she rarely took the usual next step of trying to get it published. Although she published a few poems in newspapers and obscure poetry newsletters, she was more inclined to simply file her poems once they were written and move on to something else, such as her novel writing. It should also be remembered that, as Van Duyn pointed out in her lecture (somewhat contradicting her complaint about too many people regarding themselves as poets), until the 1970s it was extremely difficult for a woman poet to get published, and the poetry world has remained male-dominated. Undoubtedly, there are many serious and talented women poets who have been unable to get their poetry published, but who are nonetheless deserving of the title of poet.

Occasionally, during the last decade or so of her life, Jean would send my two brothers and my sister copies of a poem she had composed. She sent me a copy of "Epiphany to My Son" in the late 1980s. I thanked her for it, noting that it brought back a vague memory of my first sight of the real world, if that was possible. I also expressed my concern to her over the poem's apparent suggestion that some strange relatives brought her some bottles of liquor in "brown paper packages," which she presumably drank while in labor with me in the clinic in Casper, Wyoming. She wrote back: "Egads, you took my poetic metaphors too literally — the brown paper packages were not stuff to drink, the illness and retching was a metaphor, not reality, as were the 'dark potions'" (which, she explained, were drugs given in those days to the woman "to put her out and to allow the baby to be delivered with no trouble and without the woman interfering"). That metaphor perhaps could have been made less ambiguous. In any case, these poems, grouped appropriately enough under "Family," fall into the category of domestic poetry (the category for which Van Duyn's poetry is known).

It was not until after my mother's death that I finally read through all of her poems, many for the first time. Most of her poems had been filed away haphazardly and ignored for decades. A few of these were still only handwritten. At least one, "Prayer Beads," was still unfinished. Suddenly, these poems became precious and poignant verbal embodiments of her life, her inner voice, her views, and her spirit. For me, reading many of her poems for the first time was comparable aesthetically to seeing the French paintings from the usually covetous Barnes Foundation on display at the National Gallery of Art in 1993 and discovering new masterworks of Auguste Renoir, Paul Cézanne, Van Gogh, Georges Seurat, Henri Rousseau, Pablo Picasso, and Amedeo Modigliani. As the paintings enhanced my appreciation of the work of these great artists, my mother's poems added new insights to my appreciation of her creativity and her life. Each of her poems is unique in that it captures a certain mood, emotion, idea, sense of place or time, or an event, which is essentially what a work of art does as well.

Had I read her poems as closely as I have since her death from pancreatic cancer on August 22, 1992 (the day after her seventy-seventh birthday), I would have better appreciated the life-long, hidden emotional devastation caused her by the death of her literary mother when Jean was only nine years old, and, beginning in the late 1960s, Jean's increasingly strong identification with feminism. Several of her poems, such as "Little Mother" and "A Poem for Vesta," reflect the emotional scars from her childhood that remained with her all of her life. Undoubtedly, the emotional impact of the early death of her mother with the Greek name, "the woman from Pennsylvania instead of Peloponnesus," contributed to Jean's life-long creativity. (A renowned contemporary of hers of protean creativity, Orson Welles, who like Jean was born in 1915, was also known to have suffered similar life-long grief over the death of his mother when he was nine years old.)

Jean's poems are representative of all stages of her life and her various exotic places of residence, as well as her more mundane life as a homemaker in Yellow Springs, a small college town in southwestern Ohio. She appreciated the town's identity as a literate and verdant oasis in what Eliot might have described as an intellectual wasteland, but which Jean describes in "Trace Elements" as "the midwest jungle that claims me." The town's literate identity goes back to Horace Mann's founding of Antioch College in 1852. (The bronze statue of Mann, cast in Rome in 1863 and worthy of gracing the nation's capital, stands tall but out of sight to all but occasional hikers in a secluded field in the college's Glen.) While living in Yellow Springs, Mann himself was visited by his friend Ralph Waldo Emerson. In this century, numerous writers, poets, and other creative people have lived in or visited the town.

I chose not to organize these poems in a straightforward, chronological way, wherein all poems written in a certain place and period are grouped together, not only because most of the poems were undated, but also because Jean lived in so many different countries. Furthermore, a topical arrangement, incorporating the theme of the four seasons, seemed more interesting than a simple chronological listing. It begins, after several poems on her philosophy of poetry, with childhood memories and ends with winter poems and her final foreboding yet joyful, Fellini-like poem, "Dream of the Winter Solstice." In other words, this collection of her poetry spans at least fifty-seven years of occasional poetry writing. In so doing, it chronicles her progression from the youthful exuberance of "Lyric to Life" to the brooding farewell of "Winter Solstice." It tells the story of an original American woman of the twentieth century whose intellectual, creative, social, and feminist proclivities led her, in her final years, after devoting most of her life to her selfless, often thankless roles as mother, wife, and homemaker, to serving as the first woman mayor of Yellow Springs and playing a leading role in organizing Women's Economic Assistance Ventures (WEAV), a regional affiliate of Women's World Banking, in southwestern Ohio.

Jean wrote some of her most distinctive poetry in the late 1930s and early 1940s, before she became a mother. Her romantic, lyrical poems of those decades, composed mainly in formal verse, seem to be more poetic in a classical sense than her later poems. Her earlier poems contain some lyrics that even famous poets might envy. Some of Jean's later poems, which were more often written in free verse, reflected the "love-hate relationship" that she often felt as a feminist between her conflicting needs for creative solitude and social activism. She attempted to maintain a balance between both activities, but eventually the former was crowded out by the latter, as she became more preoccupied with social and political issues. In the final chapter of her life, she seemed to be fulfilling Horace Mann's motto: "Be afraid to die until you have won some victory for humanity."

Her poems also reflect her keen intellect, her life-long pursuit of philosophical self-knowledge, her deep social and political concerns, and her acute awareness of aging and time passing, as symbolized by her inimitable descriptions of seasonal changes and time itself. They constitute a kind of journal of her views and feelings toward certain people, places, events, and *la condition humaine*. Whatever the literary significance of Jean's poems and however they come to be viewed by professional poets, these poems have given me a greater appreciation of poetry and are far more meaningful to me than most contemporary poetry that I have read.

Jean had an almost animistic feeling for nature, which she occasionally described onomatopoeically with her rich vocabulary e.g., "the sibilant tide" in "The Savage;" or metaphorically, e.g., "the forest weeps dead leaves" in "Weeping Forest;" assonantly, e.g., "lightened and brightened by the sun in the spring" in "Under the Birch Trees;" or alliteratively, e.g., "The sunlight sleeping softly" in "Meeting." The wind, in particular, evoked a wide range of emotions or memories in her poetry, from Wyoming towns to the Saudi desert. Her poetry is also pervaded with references to sunlight, sky, stars, trees, leaves, night, seasons, et cetera. Some of her youthful poems are also sprinkled with poetic words like "sundust," "stardust," and "moonglow."

Besides her original aesthetic sensibility, her deep concern for humanity, and her appreciation of nature, what stands out in Jean's poems is her acute, life-long existential awareness of the finiteness of life and her search for meaning within the context of "the immensity of time" and the "flow" of her life and time itself. In my somewhat biased opinion as a layman, whose only foray into poetry consists of having edited this volume, a number of Jean's poems are exceptionally beautiful. "Our Moment in Time" has a Shakespearean ring, whereas "Identity" has a Dalí-esque quality. Her surreal images of encountering herself on "a solitary plain" and of time "flattened" into "an elongated plain" conjure up Salvador Dalí's 1931 painting "The Persistence of Memory," which shows large watch faces melted on a bleak terrain.

The subjects of time and identity are leitmotifs of Jean's poetry. The title of this volume is taken from her phrase "the foreverness of time," which ends her longest poem, "Wyoming Legend." According to my father, the *Casper Herald Tribune* published "Wyoming Legend" on January 1, 1947, and named Jean Wyoming's poet laureate. According to *Webster's Ninth*, the word "foreverness" was coined (somewhat coincidentally) in 1945. I would not be surprised if Jean was somehow the first author to use the term, but if she was not at least she was one of the first to use it, if indeed it was coined in 1945.

Jean painted her artistic subjects with words and sentences instead of paint and brushstrokes. Counterparts to other famous paintings could be found for a number of her other poems, especially those in the Foreign Places and Autumn sections. Many of the same subjects that have inspired artists also inspired my mother the poet, e.g., the subject of "Beneath the Birches" was also Théodore Rousseau's subject in his painting "Under the Birches." Her pithy "Wind in Autumn" is an exquisite poetic equivalent of

Edvard Munch's 1893 existential painting "The Cry," which depicts a distraught woman standing on a coastal bridge against a blood-red sky, screaming with her hands covering her ears. Doubtlessly, Jean felt like the woman in the Munch painting on all too many occasions. Similar emotional stress inspired her to write "A Poem for Vesta," "Standing Alone," and "Disconnected," for example. Fortunately for my mother, the literature of feminism helped her to cope with gender injustice. (I like to think that I helped in that regard by giving her a copy of Germaine Greer's *The Female Eunuch* in 1971.)

To be sure, a few of Jean's poems puzzle me. One of her more cryptic poems, but one nonetheless rich in poetic imagery, is "Jungle," which is set in an exotic Asian locale as seen through the eyes of what may be a hunter, who is revealed somewhat inexplicably to be a man, and an animal such as a tiger. Like many of her poems, "Jungle" has a symbolic nature, but its message eluded me. If "Jungle" is a subtle feminist salvo against men, then that is about as anti-male chauvinist as her poems get. Unlike feminist poet Adrienne Rich's vitriolic depiction of men as parasitic toward women, insecure, and unworthy even of pity, the feminist-oriented poems in Jean's volume seem mild by comparison. Only four or five of Jean's poems — "Driven Woman," "Mask-Making Workshop," "Sisterhood," "The Coldest Winter," and "The Elements of Verbal Subjugation" — reflect her feminist ethos. Also unlike Rich's poems, Jean's are for the most part nonpolitical. Only about three of her poems, grouped in the Protest section, have an angry political orientation. (A life-long Democrat, Jean was active in the peace movement.) Jean identified, however, with Rich's "I am an instrument in the shape of a woman trying to translate pulsations into images for the relief of the body and the reconstruction of the mind." (I know because Jean underlined the quote in her copy of *The Quotable Woman*.)

Although my mother died gracefully, smiling her warm smile almost to the end, she was not ready to go quite so soon. She was especially looking forward to writing her autobiography, as if to prove that one need not be famous to have a life worth writing about. Her autobiography would have been of particular interest to her family and many friends. Sadly, however, Jean's cancer deprived her of her once boundless and seemingly indefatigable creativity and strength, before she got beyond writing the outline. Thus, it is left for her poems to provide poignant vignettes of her life-story by conveying her thoughts and feelings about some of the people, places, and events that mattered to her or otherwise made an impression, be it positive or negative. Her family members and many friends are especially fortunate that she left this wealth of poems, which will help to preserve her memory and her unique, poetic vision of life and the world. It is of great consolation that she lived a full life. As she wrote in 1939 in "Lyric to Life," when she was twenty-four, "I have lived with the beautiful, and I have loved it long."

Jean's later poems also convey the gloomier outlook that she had in her final years, as the aging process took an increasing emotional toll on her. A case in point is her final poem, "Dream of the Winter Solstice." But even that poem retained a glimmer of the joy of "Lyric to Life" and of her own essentially joyful, albeit contemplative, personality. The poem ends, after-all, on a haiku note. She brought joy to family and friends alike—whether through her kindness and graciousness, her warm personality, her intellectual, creative, social, and feminist perspectives, her deep concern for the world, her always sympathetic ear as mother or friend, her gourmet cooking, et cetera—and the publication of her poems should help to preserve the memory of her joyful legacy. Indeed, the word "joy" seems to sum up her life and her philosophy of life. One of her final poetic images was, appropriately enough, the word JOY hanging in the sky, perhaps sparkling like a Fourth of July fireworks display. (Her reference to "bonfires in the sky" in "Winter Solstice" is an allusion to the nighttime mountainside bonfires of Ecuadorian peasants on Pichincha, the volcano that towers over Quito, and under which we lived.) For me and undoubtedly for others who knew and loved Jean, these poems will be a testament to her joy, as well as her anger at the world's injustices, and they will keep her name lit up brightly in our memories. Perhaps the publication of her poems will also allow them to be read and appreciated a hundred years hence by someone who, seeking a few moments of retrospective respite from a far less habitable world teeming with billions of people, happens to come across a tattered copy of the volume.

Rex A. Hudson
Falls Church, Virginia
July 4, 1993

PROLOGUE

by

Jean Barlow Hudson

THE ACTIVIST woman poet is a divided person. Within her are siblings whose love-hate relationship neither of them can do without. The activist feeds the longing of the poet for solitude, for the flowing spring of creativity; a conflict builds to a fever pitch of excitement and need. The poet feels both starved and enriched. Enriched because the activity, mental and physical, is invigorating, and the human contacts and the defining of values molds the poet's stockpile of material. In a way, one could say it is like the building of a compost heap that will eventually enrich the soil of the garden. Yet the poet imagines, and it may be that it is truly so, that poems are being lost, that creativity has seeped away unused and will never return. The poet is starved for time to dream, for written verification on the page that she exists.

The activist feels that sister-poet gives to her; she has visions of what could be, she is sensitive to earth and to people, she is sensitive to need, and the creativity of the poet feeds into her bloodstream energy and exuberance. Alas, she is also nettled by the nagging demands of sister-poet, who wants to shut herself away to forget her responsibility for the rest of the world.

Fulfillment comes from both activities, both modes of being. Yet the conflict does not cease. The poet-activist is torn and bleeding, strangled by her own accomplishments, indulgences, and sacrifices. Being able to explain and understand her conflict makes it easier to bear. She becomes a husk, blown about in the wind. She feels she is not taken seriously; she feels she is taken too seriously. She wonders if she has trivialized her own lifework. But suddenly there can be a breakthrough, a truce, perhaps, or an unexpected release of energy and accomplishment, and the dry husk becomes once more a fat, pregnant grain, growing, producing. Then, after the birth of a new work, there is a reconciliation between the sibling rivals. The cycle begins again.

1

*   *   *

There are many kinds of poetry: the poetry of rhyme, the image poem, the narrative poem, the love poem, the ballad. John Ciardi has said that "the concern is not to arrive at a definition...but to arrive at an experience." Yet we ask ourselves, how can I experience a poem? Sometimes it does not speak to me at all. This is just it, I think. All poems will not communicate to all of us. But surely there are some poems that will communicate a world of experience to someone.

The words in our language acquire either a prosaic, a neutral, or a frightening dire connotation. Others acquire connotations that pull out of our thoughts associations of pleasure, of dreams, even inspiration. There are words that sound like music, words that sound like motion. My own preference is for strong rhythms in poems, for interesting groups of sounds, and for words and combinations of words that release my own inner dialogue.

Poetry doesn't concern itself with facts, and sometimes there is little external meaning to a poem, rather an inner dialogue of connotations so that it gives us an experience much the same as a piece of music. Sometimes a poem has a symbolic nature to it: it seems to be telling one story, but underneath another is being told.

There is a body involvement in sounding words that becomes a distinct part of the word's message. For instance, the word "elate" feels one way and "thud" feels another. So also for clack, alleluia, ululate, majestic, crunch.

When you get down to it, you read or listen to a poem and then say, "I like it," or you say, "I don't like it." The poem probably didn't communicate to you if you didn't like it.

I

ON POETRY

On Poetry

Poetry is born from tendrils of thought,
remembered fragments thought-blown, thistle-down,
of straying senses.
Poetry is trace of tears, the broken edge of laughter
caught in the barbed memory of yesterday.
Even like the last breath departing from a song
hung to the mute melody that hovers forever
on the soul's abyss.
And all of this, heart-garnered, deciphered,
and flung to the pencil-point of time.

The Poetry of Living

Poetry is not of the words only.
Poetry is in the deeds accomplished,
in life's adventures.
There are poems in children's faces
that cannot be spoken or penned.
There are poems in men's works,
when there is love and honor
in the labor itself, or the task complete.
There are sonnets in a woman's kitchen
as she moves in the day's ritual,
speaking no words, thinking no coherent thoughts.
Yet the heart's intentions and the hand's obedience
make verses of singular beauty.

Poems make a carpet that lies across the days
and up the steps of night, so that the lyrics
lovers utter soundlessly stand side by side
with the poetry coming from solitude
and thoughts standing serene and alone.
The carpet stretches and meets in the dawn
of the day again and unwinds increasingly
into poetry of hours ahead as yet unlived,
the unending ritual of work and play
and thought and passion.
Poetry is of living and is not found
on the page alone.

II

CHILDHOOD

Carnival Boy

Delaware, Ohio, late 1930s

The carnival train has come to town,
all painted red and orange and brown.
And from our yard when I'm at play
I watch the carnival people across the way.

And while I was playing with my toys,
a big fat carnival lady with one of the boys
came up our street to go to the grocery store
to buy a couple bottles of pop or more.

The lad was ragged and dirty and shy,
and I smiled at him as he went by.
He put his hand on my brand new trike,
and I said, "You can ride it if you like."

But his ma jerked him on as cross as could be
and said for him not to bother folks like me.
I wished she'd let the ragged carnival boy
stay and play awhile with my fine new toy.

Calliope

Delaware, late 1930s

Oh, what do I love more than all my toys,
more than Mummy or Daddy, or girls and boys,
more than all fine things on land or sea?
Why, it's the calliope, the calliope!

Oh, what would I follow wherever it led,
run faster to follow than trains have sped?
And when I grow bigger what would I be?
Why, the man at the wheel of the calliope!

And what do I hear when at night I lie down
and everyone's sleeping all over the town?
Why, the faraway, soft-away, only-for-me
call of the circus calliope, calliope!

Puppet

Delaware, late 1930s

I am but a puppet upon life's puppet stage,
and the hand that moves behind me is the God
that rules my days.
At his command, I shake my head
and vigorously gesticulate,
or sink in stupid lethargy across the playhouse gate.
He moves again. I take a step, and with a pompous stride
across the stage I hurry, my destiny prescribed.

I am but a puppet upon life's puppet stage,
and when the children laugh and shout
to see my clownish ways
I nod my waggish head and wave my padded paw,
for to reveal my master is to desecrate the law.
Just when my aching sawdust soul is planning on escape,
the hand behind me jerks again.
I bow, I flop, I scrape,
and the little children scream
at how strange it is to see a puppet
who can clown and strut in such unheard-of liberty.

Deserted

Delaware, late 1930s

What happens to the carnival when it goes away?
Where is the merry-go-round I rode the other day?
The field is all empty, the air is sad and still.
Where is the music that followed me over the hill?

Where are the balloon men, the cotton candy stall,
the hotdog and Coke men, the popcorn and all?
I've looked up and down the highway;
I've watched the early trains.
Won't the carnival find its way to come back again?
I asked my mother but she only shook her head
and told me to find my doll and play with her instead.
Yet I only want the merry-go-round. Where did it go?
Why did it go away when it knew I loved it so?

Make-Believe

Delaware, late 1930s

He is no more. And so
I pretend, as a half-fey child,
that all is well,
and people my world with
paper dolls of great
importance, and build
real castles and
modern houses out
of sand; until I
half-believe that all
of them really
exist.

Dawn Kiss

Golden, Colorado, early 1940s

Like a country morning in June
with the dew tips on the timothy,
and the field birds singing among the wild cherry,
like this, ay, like the quintessence of a thousand
such mornings, was your first kiss.

I can feel it now
(and the salt tear of remembrance stings on my tongue).
So gently, tenderly given by your young boy's mouth
trembling a little.
Our lips pressing ever so lightly,
then withdrawing quickly,
awed by the magic that touched us.
And smiling together there in the darkness,
you took my hand and quoted, while we walked
up the quiet street,
"The red rose is a falcon, the white rose is a dove. . . ."

Oh, boy-lover, come back, come back.
Lay your love shyly upon me once more.
Let us pass up that same street
and feel again the dawn-kiss of our lives.

Little Mother

The winds of winter are crying at your window,
little mother. Its icy fists are tearing, beating at your window
in wild, macabre glee.
The breath of winter is creeping in your pain-racked
chamber, little mother, and plays upon your counterpane
in mocking ecstasy.

The night's dark hours are eons in a row,
and eerie Faustian fancies come and go.
No voice, but a hound dog's bay
and slow, deep pain to wait with until the day.

The spring's handmaid is waiting in the lane,
little mother.
The robin in her hand is throating,
and she holds April in her eyes.
Beneath the ice and snow, the garden loam is waking,
little mother.
The lonely crow remembers wild cherry blossoms
and rain-washed skies.

The winter's wind has reached the flame;
with one last cry death made its claim.
Now thought and pain are blended into one;
the battle of the will and flesh is lost.

The wind moaned on the hilltop where they laid you,
little mother, and the snow fell gently,
in deep repentance,
to crystallize our tears.
The spring's handmaid came up the lane and missed you,
little mother, and pledged her heart to restitute for
winter, through all the years.

16

A Poem for Vesta

Yellow Springs, Ohio, 1970s

There is a story I've tried to tell again and again,
finding the words jam in my throat, extending
their iron down through my guts.
It's the death of a woman I'm trying to relate.
My mother.
It was a mistake.
She knew it was not supposed to be.
She was not trained to fight; accepted pliantly the
knife, the radiation that doctors ordered; finally
accepted her fate.
For God's sake, you'd think
I could deal with this after all the years.
You'd think I could pick over the fragile bones
of her death with detachment, as if she had been a woman
from the history of early Greece—one of the vestal maidens
buried in the sacred grove who in her time
had borne children to a warrior who went on
a sea voyage to Carthage and never returned;
she became a priestess, served the Goddess,
succumbed, perhaps, to a plague and died.

You see, it is easy to fantasize; there were clues
she left to support the story: her profile classic,
her Greek name, her grace and spirituality.
But the real person, my mother—the woman who lived
in Pennsylvania instead of Peloponnesus—is the ghost
who haunts me, refusing to be forgotten.
She refused death, fought it like a warrior,
until it took her by force, squeezing the last drop
of endurance from the battered frame
before our eyes and ears.
All right. It happened.
As a child, I was gravely hurt,
as if a spear had pierced my body,
missing vital parts.
I grew weighted with scar tissue.
I wonder now if a wild dance with rituals,

17

cymbals, and drums could have emptied and cleansed
my grief; an orgy around her winter grave,
shrieks and wails, the rending of garments.
We were mute and passive.
We spoke little of grief in our family.
Like inert fish in the frozen pond,
we held sorrow inside.
The snow-covered Allegheny hills closed around us,
locking our throats, solidifying sorrow.
Mother, Vesta, woman of my flesh, our points are narrowing.
When my anger and loss flow into the stream of life,
will you be exorcised and both of us set free?

Stillwater Creek

Delaware, late 1930s

There is a spring I shall remember.
There is a place I cannot forget.
There is a June so far, so young, so tender
that I can taste (and touch the day) even yet.

There is a creek I used to wander
whose icy waters raced swift and deep
out through the crust of snow.

III

COLLEGE

Lyric to June

Delaware, 1935

With hungry arms, I try to catch
June fast slipping past.
I want to hold its loveliness
longer than the lovely last.

I want to keep June mornings,
so fresh and bright and young.
I want to keep June daytimes,
fast sinking with the sun.

I want to hold its shadows,
which come creeping in with eve'.
A June moon smiles more tender,
for June moons never grieve.

I want this month of promise
to linger longer still,
for it gives me more hope
than all the others will.

Desolation

Delaware, 1936

A star shone bright in its circled orb.
I used to watch it there.
A light flashed down, a streak of gold,
that place in the sky was bare.

A pine tree lay against the sky,
pointing its way, and my way too.
A storm came by, the lightning flashed.
Now there's only a space in the blue.

A song fell out in tumbled notes
from a cheerful sparrow by my door.
An eagle swooped and clutched its prey.
The song has ceased; it is no more.

Love tripped in and ruled my heart.
Happiness had triumphant reign.
But on my joy a shadow fell,
and now my love has gone again.

Lyric to Life

Delaware, 1936

Why should I not wear a rapturous look
and my heart always carry a song?
For I have lived with the beautiful,
and I have loved it long.

I have lain in the arms of sweet-smelling earth,
and whistled along with the bird.
I have walked in the depths of intimate night.
The voice of the wind and rain I have heard.

I have awoke and praised the beautiful dawn.
I have laughed and run to meet the days.
I have told a secret to silent blue hills.
They have whispered to me why the pine tree sways.

I have sat by the bank of the rushing stream.
I have lingered and bathed in its flow.
They left me legends of the fox and deer.
They told me tales of the lands they know.

That's why my heart is overflowing with praise
and my lips almost bursting with song.
For I have lived with the beautiful,
and I have loved it long.

The Star Folk I

Delaware, 1937

I come dreaming by your door
with stardust in my eyes
and moonglow for my cloak.
I come bringing beauty by
for all you lovely folk.

I bring a bag of laughter.
I bring a bag of tears.
I'll sprinkle love drops in your eyes
and sing a song of years.

Oh, look for me at twilight,
and look for me at dawn.
And sing a dreamsong of your own,
when I have passed and gone.

Star Folk II

Delaware, 1937

Hie you, you in my moonbed,
you in the silvery gown,
you with the dreamy smile
playing about your lips,
come you down!

Oh, kind sir, please stay your wrath
and bid me linger here.
When my star crumbled, down I fell
and this soft bed was here.

O, sing you pixies,
dance, you gnomes.
Play your reeds and sing.
The moon-king has taken a wife,
and the star-lady found a king.

Love in the Springtime

Delaware, 1938

Oh, love me much in the springtime,
when the bud of our love is new.
Stay with me all of these careless days
when the vows we make are true.

For there will come in the summer,
in the maddening light of the moon,
the crest of love as it bursts its bud
and blossoms all too soon.

And I fear the flame of autumn,
with its swiftly changing days,
for love may pattern all too well
and die out with their blaze.

And the winter mocks a lover's pact
with a frozen purity
that hides the dead and sunken flame
of love's maturity.

So, love me much in the springtime
when all the world is kind,
and nature, too, is spinning dreams
and faith itself is blind.

Entreaty in Autumn

Delaware, 1937

Sing a poem into my ears, autumn bird,
of something new or old.
Draw that poem into thyself, most inner heart,
and write it there in gold.

Blow a poem into my lips, autumn wind,
in litany or lyric.
Speak that poem into my life, my soul,
that all the world may hear it.

Leafless Tree

Delaware, 1937

I met you by the side of the road
upon a hill one winter afternoon.
I loved your splendid nakedness,
and even spring could come too soon.
        Leafless tree!

Each outlined sprig and jutted bough
lifted reverent hands to God,
a lovely offering unadorned.
I, in silence, thee applaud.
        Leafless tree!

The sun shines silver on your bark,
such beauty — silver, black, and blue.
So proud you stand, so simplified.
I, no fairer hope to view.
        Leafless tree!

Study Hour

Delaware, 1938

The wood fire crackles and the clock
is chasing little minutes with a tock.
The sky without is closing up the day,
drawing down the curtains, mauve and grey.

And now before I settle down
with Ben Jonson or Sir Thomas Browne,
I say a magic word and wave my pen
and shout "Come on, darling, hurry in!"

Then, swish, space has vanished in midair,
and darling's here beside my chair.
Oh, my pen is true and will not tell
the secrets that it knows too well.
So we must skip to now from then
when I'm alone once more with Brown and Ben.

Lament of a Sculptor's Model

Delaware, 1938

They slap me up in plaster,
and they shape me into clays.
I am born of a thousand artists
and shaped in as many ways.

They cast me into forms of bronze.
They chisel me in steel.
I don't care if I'm shaped in dung
if it means another meal.

I pray, I dance, I leap, I run,
and I learn to cower in fear.
I wear the face of a nun in prayer;
I give them the harlot's leer.

They say I'm the perfect figure
since de Milo quit the modeling game.
They hang my bust in Carnegie Hall,
my legs in the Hall of Fame.

I've heard I'm art's gift to creation.
Yet this highbrow stuff gets me down.
I'd toss it all if some chirp in the chips
got me a flat on the far side of town.

Litany

Delaware, late 1930s

Oh, no, dear heart, I do not mourn.
My well of tears has long since ceased its flow.
Nor do I visit now with sprays of flowers
wherein they laid you—it's better so.

Nor do I now seclude myself from throngs,
nor discipline my mind from thoughts of you.
The open wound has mended now with time;
I am laughing now the way I used to do.

And yet, though you have passed beyond,
and though I may appear to wander free,
a cloak invisible around me clings
the shadow that your love left over me.

Often when I am knelt in worship
in the quiet holiness of some temple shrine,
I sense another form close kneeling;
I feel a prayer of yours arise with mine.

I find myself watching a pair of hands
that must have the same familiar grace
with which they work or lay at rest,
and I see you there in someone's place.

And although I should learn to love
another heart, brave, sweet, and true,
and if our hearts become as one,
if I should build my life anew—

I know, as surely as I know the time,
if I should let my heart speak clear
and close my eyes and silent be,
the beating of your heart in mine I'd hear.

30

I'd know that all my other loves
were but precious children of our own.
Sprung from one deep eternal love
that can never leave my heart alone.

IV

SPRINGTIME IN WARTIME

The Approaching Calamity

Delaware, 1938

"War?" they say, "Oh, it won't break
until the spring.
Hitler's last speech was milder,
and Chamberlain parleys with Benito and Bonnet.
War won't break until the spring."

Until the spring, until the spring.
War won't break until the spring.
When winter lifts her last caress
and April trips in wantonness
across the country's nakedness.
Oh, death won't come until the spring.

"France is buying bombers,
and Britain is maneuvering her fleet.
The president is begging for more submarines.
National defense must prepare to meet
the approaching calamity by the spring."

Until the spring, until the spring.
They grant us life until the spring.
Beauty bursting on orchard boughs;
lovers whispering their first vows.
With fresh delights the land endows,
but death will be here by the spring.

"Our country, first in the air and the sea,"
is now the creed of every man.
A mobilized youth, a mechanized world
will merge at the spurt of the flame,
and none will predict beyond the spring.

Beyond the spring, beyond the spring.
None will predict beyond the spring.
The blossom of this bud we hold,

35

will we not see it then unfold?
Or is life but a dream we're told,
because there's no peace
beyond the spring?

Specter of Spring

Golden, early 1940s

Something in the face of spring this year is changed.
It seems withdrawn and cold,
clinging to the skirts of winter.
Her eyes are hollow, dark, and strange;
her white hand tightly clinched.

I think it is because the boys are gone
(it was to them the spring belonged).
With guns they plow this year,
with instruments of death they till the land.
They do not sing while they work this spring;
their mouths are set and grim.

The woods are empty of their wild glad shouts.
The streets are sober, echoing the quick footstep,
the untamed cry of strong boys drunk with the joy
of a new season.
The nights are silent; everywhere there is remembering.

Here in the peaceful fields, the loam turns over slowly,
sighing for the young, the springing step
that does not come;
missing the strong sure touch on the plow,
turning a straight furrow.
Dry are the seeds this spring though the rains fall,
and the air is warm.

The March wind is springtime
(do you hear it in the trenches?),
soughing over a sterile land where women lie alone
and finger the empty pillow, dreaming uncertain dreams.

Give us back the winter; lay it deep and cold.
Let its icy fingers sting.
We are too haunted by this thin specter of a season
wandering over a lonely land bereft of husbanding.

Morning Sky

Golden, early 1940s

The morning sky is restless, and the clouds move
back and forth, until they find
some cool retreat beneath the edge of day.
The early sky is deep and brilliant in its blue,
before the sun has climbed
the rungs of gold that lead unto the zenith hour.
Restless too the trees; they flutter nervously
against the unknown noon.
The cottonwoods turn silver stomachs to the wind
that passes lightly and swiftly from morning hour to hour,
until each taste and touch of night is lifted,
and the shining day stands eager and unhidden like some
newly opened flower.

Beneath the Birches

I lie and watch white birch trees greening in the spring.
I watch the sun lighten and brighten the leaves
of the white birch trees greening in the spring.
And the wind blows this way and that
the greening leaves of white birch trees,
lightened and brightened by the sun in the spring.
And the still blue sky is a canopy for the white birch trees,
with the greening leaves tossed this way and that by the wind
and lightened and brightened by the sun in the spring.
And the wooded hills encircle the white birch trees
with the greening leaves lightened and brightened by the sun
and tossed this way and that by the wind and canopied
by the small blue sky in the spring.
And the lake ripples and reflects the encircling hills
beneath the still blue sky that canopies the white birch trees,
with the greening leaves lightened and brightened by the sun
and tossed this way and that by the wind in the spring.
And I rise and move into the ring of white birch trees.
I raise my hands and lift my voice and project my command,
but the wind tosses my voice this way and that.
The white birch trees with the greening leaves are still
lightened and brightened by the sun, blown by the wind, framed
by the wooded hills, canopied by the still blue sky,
and reflected in the mirror of the lake that ripples and moves
this way and that in the spring.

Bereft of Poetry

Casper, Wyoming, late 1940s

It is gone, fled, untraceable. . . .
The poetry in which my soul had sung
its way from year to year.
Gone with the break of the guns
and the march of the uniformed men.

It would seem that poetry would thrive,
being speech to man's emotions.
Indeed, it would seem that passionless verse
would become mighty with passion,
great in its wrath — deep, deep in its grief.

But there is utter silence now within my soul
and a long, long wondering.

To a Brother on the Frontline

Golden, 1944

We have only your picture now, little brother,
and the news on the radio,
and the hope that you will return
from that distant, unknown island
to your green and happy home.

We have only your picture, splendid in dress uniform.
Yet I see not the braid, or the blue, or the silver
buttons, but that part which is you, and the remembrance
of you emanating from it.

I would use the word "beautiful," yet I hear
your laugh and your scorn.
I would use the word "princely," for no crown
or no breeding could make you more royal.
But you are a simple country boy, and this is the truth.
Too young and too innocent for the war that has caught you.
Guiltless of the wrong that is done you,
so young and unsustained,
virginal, too, a child in your teens.

What then shall I say to your picture?
Shall I say there never was a youth with gaze
so clear, so true, so honest?
Never a face so sweet, so tender-young?
Never eyes so large and calm, hiding some luminous
thought,
never brows so dark and heavy, mouth so straight,
but with the smile waiting on the underlip?

I remember you, brother, in the same thought with
farmlands, green and growing,
orchards, barns, grainfields, and timber lands,
and the sweet woods and the October hunt.
I remember you, brother, the country boy, loving
your life, and proud,

and the pride is there, sitting erect on your shoulders,
and the chin lifted.

What do they see, those eyes, looking so levelly
over my shoulder?
Not, I know, the battlefield, nor the stiffened
corpses, nor the bomb craters,
nor the palms on that strange Pacific island,
nor the surf beating endlessly throughout the tropic night,
nor the beachhead littered with cannon,
and the barges moving out,
and the endless line of the ocean, the enemy zone.

What do those eyes see? Do they see the farm
and the village?
The fields you loved to roam?
Do they see blue Allegheny hills?
Or do those eyes dream of your girl, the wind-blown
country girl, whom you left with a promise,
and remember sharply, carrying her now
in the innermost fold of your wallet,
yet remembering the toss of her hair,
and how she hunted with you in the autumn.

There are those at home who pray for you,
pray that you return.
But, brother, I cannot pray, I cannot pray.
I can only sit here before your picture, my heart
wrenched, and the memory of you becoming an anguish too deep
to utter, too deep to bear.

Wild Bird

Golden, early 1940s

O Wild Bird, scion of the earth and sea;
tormented one, unbound, yet never, never free;
unbidden prisoner, unplanned, unasked,
unhoped-for destiny.
Where are you, Wild Bird?
Lost child of this mad century.

This land you wandered, yet it was never home;
this sea you sailed sent death shells through the foam;
the song you offered wistfully transposed into a moan.
Where are you, Wild Bird?
Where in this endless maze? Where do you roam?

Too young this world's catastrophe has taught you
life is the jealous mistress, she's the master, too;
and she's no gracious lady, she's a back-turned shrew.
Where are you, Wild Bird?
Where in this ambush have they trapped you?

Seagulls Over an Inland Field

San Diego, early 1940s

Why come you, white seagulls, dipping and soaring
over the barren stubble of an inland field?
Why have you left white wavecaps, the gleaming foam,
and sea-bright air to wander on some nameless quest
through the wood and alien field?
In here where skies and soil must, voiceless, tasteless,
be of all the ways of home?

Go back, wild birds!
Whatever it is you seek so far,
it will not recompense be for the high salt spume,
for the waves beating upon the reefs,
the leap and plunge of sea life,
the sands bleached by the kisses of the spray.
Go back, before the grip of home is hurting,
and you have flown too far, too far away!

Warning to a World at War

Golden, early 1940s

Some year, oh world, the spring will stay a frozen hope
within the breast of winter,
held fast by arctic ice, sealed in algid marble,
a bulging tumor and an overgrowth of winter.
Too long, too long, the spring has come, fresh,
untouched and innocent.
Too long held forth fertility to meet a sterile world.
Soil will not mix with abortive blood, fresh from
the veins of workers.
This earth will not yield anew each year into a morass of hate.
Birth must meet birth, not leap into the arms of death.
Fallow land must have seed, and the toil of men at peace.
Not these tortured plantings of shrapnel, steel,
and the rotting flesh of children.

The World's Future

Golden, 1944

Will the poetry be saved, and the music score,
when the rot takes over and the worms begin to bore?
Or will they all—Beethoven, Rembrandt, Shakespeare,
Schiller—be shoveled under with the dung as filler?
And will that future being (purplish, nebulous in imagination)
who takes over when we ignobly have lost our station
start out his little destiny with the culture
of the anthropoid and time to them a darkness,
mysterious and void?
Then could we not prepare a little packet
guaranteed against decay or some monster's crude hatchet
to hold some samples of our music, literature, and art
to witness to the ages, and give future man a helpful start?
Or could it be that the cultural fruits
we'd leave hanging on the tree
would carry taint of our diseases on to eternity?
Better to let the new seed start out naked in the ground
with naught but the simple elements pure and unprofound
to attend the birth. So we, then sleeping fitfully,
will not bear guilt of more than our own destiny.

V

LOVE

Eternal Love

Golden, early 1940s

I dreamed last night, when the night was still,
and there were none stirring in home or mill,
that our two souls a-wandering went,
wherever the roads of the world were bent.
We passed through cities, street after street;
we passed through fields and where crossroads meet.
And to all whom we met, we spoke the same word
and shook our heads at the answers we heard.
Searching, inquiring, looking deep into faces,
we spoke to all men, paused at all places.
And to each we said: "We are two lovers; this is our love.
Tell us, do you know, anyplace on earth or above,
is there anything of more beauty, more value, more bliss
that you have seen which compares to this?"

Some brought out riches to dazzle our eyes,
while others had answers profound and wise.
Some took us at sunset to behold the West,
saying "There lies the beauty that is the best."
Some led us to books and to abstract art,
saying pure beauty lay alone and apart.
Others led us to battlefields and pointed to death
to prove that beauty and sacrifice belong in one breath.
With others we interviewed men of great name,
who compared our love with notoriety and fame.

Yet hand in hand our two souls wandered by,
observing the people, the land, and the sky;
and much we beheld that was great and good
(and some evil hidden like the worm in the wood).
Yet none on the earth, beneath the moon or the sun
made by man himself or that God had done,
neither created by artist with human hand
nor sprung from fundamental air, sea, and land
could compare with the beauty, the rapture, the bliss
that you and I, love, have found in this;

our spirits, strangely met, strangely blended
yet united eternally until time too has ended.
And the book is sealed and all has been finished;
even then, even then lives our love undiminished.

Transcontinental

San Diego, 1941

Clip-clopping, he and I up the creaky stairs
to the second-floor hotel, the restaurant Golden Pheasant,
and the secondhand store underneath.
The sputum on the stairs,
tobacco juice, a butt or two,
dirt and stains from men in shabby suits who come and go,
the women passing, dime-store perfume,
bargain-counter dresses in loud prints,
they come and go.

"Rooms one dollar," the clerk says
(his look smearing us up and down).
"Attractive price, just our price, darling,
one dollar per night."
That, of course, does not mean private bath and shower.
Means a toilet down the hall with a leaky water closet.
Bed hard, blankets smelly, yet the sheets are clean and fresh.

Dark room, window on an alley, almost touch the bricks across.
Sounds of restaurant kitchen, four a.m., crates thrown down,
garbage pails clanging,
screen door banging,
voices cross, smell of cantaloupe, bacon grease, and flies.

Remember the hotel in Dallas, darling?
Man in the next room coughed all night.
Night of the big Sugar Bowl game. Why did we hit town
that night, New Year's night?
Dinner in the cafe with yellow leather seats, florescent lights.
We tried the enchiladas, and didn't we have wine?

We walked the New Year's streets, so many people,
so many noisy, laughing, wonderful people.
And we saw a cheap burlesque (lonely men beside us,
men with lost, furtive faces and whiskey breaths).
The vaudeville—dirty jokes, girls with painted
old-woman faces, the gags corny—but the men laughed.

And then again the hotel, the man coughing,
and you and I in each other's arms,
as the bells and horns and laughter resounded
in the streets below.
In the next room, the man coughed all night.

Remember the Salt Lake City room?
We looked so long; it was so crowded.
"No rooms," "nothing," "sorry" . . . suitcases so heavy.
Why did I bring so much?
And then at last a room, but so dark and dirty.
I almost couldn't stay.
Children, brat children, crying, sniffling in the hall;
toilet out of order, one said gents, one ladies;
bathtub across the hall.
Yet we made love, and the sound of the children's
snarling died away . . . so far away.

Darling, we have made love in many cities—Denver,
Chicago, Frisco, and L.A.
We have molded our imprint
on many vagrant beds of sin.
We have turned the friendship of days
into the ardor of many nights.
We have carried our small ragged pile of worldly goods
through many doorways, and set them down,
and carried them out again, to travel on
the smiling highways of the land.

We wrote on a highway sign: "Dark is the night
from pole to pole. . . ."

Oleander Bush

Casper, late 1940s

In the warm darkness, the oleander blossom
lifts its face to kiss the night.
In the dampness of night, I kiss you passionately,
not to find passion's depth, nor indeed, to find you,
but to seek my soul, which eludes me,
as the secret of its being eludes the oleander,
reaching out in the stillness and the heavy night.

Seedless Ecstasy

Golden, early 1940s

What, love, all this ecstasy
and no seed planted?
All this unleashed joy and vigor,
each to each,
and no child growing?

There must be issue from the flesh
that mingles in such splendid passion.
There must be babe to grow into a man
carrying our love in his bone's marrow,
in his heart's creation.

Woman at the Window

Golden, 1944

It is growing late, and the early evening
plays in purple slippers in the street.
There is one crimson ribbon in her hair
seen at the dark rim of the sky.
Housetops and roof lines grow black as ink,
and soft lights appear behind drawn curtains.
Still you do not come.

I kneel by the window watching,
wondering who it is that keeps you.
Who is now the reciprocator of your smile,
your voice, your strong hand's pressure?

Soft, stray breezes whisk up and down the street,
teasing at the skirts of a woman passing by.
An automobile flashes past on its secret errand.
A door is slammed with such finality.

I turn back to my room. The familiar outlines
of furniture are vague and velvety in the dusk.
There is only the purr of the fire,
and the waiting, waiting.
When will you come?

The Watcher

Golden, early 1940s

I am forever looking out of windows watching for you.
When the sunlight strikes the snow with silver splendor
or sinks into the golden green of summer lawns,
I am forever standing at the window waiting for you.
The long day deepens and again I look to the empty street.
The dusk comes in with a crimson taper
and lights the evening lamps.
It seems that all lovers have returned
to their beloveds but mine.
I stand at the window waiting, watching; will you come?
Then unaware I find I am staring into darkness
and the thin cold night is here.
The window sends back my own wistful image staring at me.
But when I turn dismayed to another night without you,
I remember, darling, that you always come . . . you always come.

Meeting

Golden, early 1940s

The wind, the wind that wanders here and there.
The sunlight sleeping softly in your hair.
The look that lingers and the touch that lays
a scarlet streak of madness, and the blood obeys.
Time that lets a moment sear deeply into space,
and memory rushing past me leaves a scar upon the place.
The step on the path has broken, broken in the spell,
and your withdrawing shadow leaves me cool-deep as a well.

Desertion

Casper, late 1940s

I shall have tea tonight when I dine;
I shall have muffins and fritters and broccoli.
The choice is mine; there will be no other across from me.
I am the guest and I am the host;
I am the husband and the wife.
You may wander, my love, I shall not mind.
I shall have tea tonight, and fritters and broccoli.

The lamplight that falls on my plate is devoid of shadow.
There is no movement of beautiful hands breaking the bread,
no smiling grey eyes when I look up.
Ah, there is a bitterness in my cup.

Primary Palette

Yellow Springs, 1970s

I am to blue, as an empty afternoon whose silence
is broken with voices hooked in the earlobes of memory;
embraced by smog, avoiding the viewless window,
yet grasping at images moving in the mists.
I am to blue.

I am to yellow, as the childlike heart
races in ecstasy toward a balloon
climbing with helium energy to an intimate universe.
In summer the saffron flower stares unblinking at the sun,
heedless of wind or the cruel scythe.
I am to yellow.

I am to red (*momento raro*).
Raceless, I touch you; depthless, I plunge.
Humanity passes to touch and kiss the common stone.
We speak—we speak with speech unheard,
eyes meeting, lips moving, sounds lost in knowledge
caught and held between us, like blood that cannot be held
when veins are opened and we lie in a common place.
I am to red.

57

The Savage

Yellow Springs, 1970s

You who know the savage,
when that time has come
you are wake and ready, though
your tongue, your wit, be numb;
you hold the door against him,
claim the wind, the stranger, the foe,
yet his cruel, sweet touch
is the one last touch
you wait to know.
You who know the savage
find in that face a friend,
and those you love and wept for
are shadowed and wan and dim;
your savage, your lover,
has come at last,
brought by the sibilant tide;
he'll carry you out to the sea again
as whole, as white as the shell on the sand.

Quiet Love

Golden, 1944

Sometimes I love you quietly,
like the seed that lies in the ground;
it loves still the sun, but awaits the day
when its blossoms shall bloom and be found.

Sometimes my love is motionless,
as the star appears in the sky;
yet steadily bent on its orbit of light
it moves eternally onward unseen by the eye.

Sometimes my love is mute and dumb,
and you question my heart if I care;
but as the song that leaves a singing throat,
it moves silently on over the waves of the air.

Fret not, dear love, if I kiss not your lips,
and you feel we are eons apart;
for the times when I love you quietly,
I hold you most close, most deep in my heart.

VI

THE HEART

Heart of the Matter

Yellow Springs, 1970s

The heart, when it is sad and strange,
speaks not with reason nor responds
to argument, logical and true.
Its pain cannot be comforted with facts
that anchor in the past.
Its speech is speechless,
and its need is needless, yet how great
its need, how vast its speech, and if not caught,
how endless is its depth of pain.

Perverse and stubborn though my heart may seem,
baffling to your honest mind, yet
leave it not to blind dismay
until some climax forces it to havoc.
Pain its own priority brings, and surely
you must know that only you can penetrate
its maze by open offering of your love.
Given once was not enough, nor twice, nor thrice,
but again, again, and again, not feeling words
too foolish nor acts too amateur or old, nor that vows
once made still bind without their repetition.

The heart, when it is sad and strange,
speaks not with reason, nor responds
to pity nor to tender kindliness,
nor lives on memories of the past.
Its need is present, potent, sure, and its pain
untouched and endless until you stoop and heal again.

A Done Deed

Casper, late 1940s

How can I tell you I will stick the knife
deep into your flesh and turn the blade
without the help of anesthesia?
How can I tell you when I love you
in a way you will not understand?

How can you comprehend me and the thing I do?
When you are left to pace a lonely room
and think of visions shattered
by a woman's deed?

I hope you know that this is part of my pain —
the pain and quiet that I must bear.
It went out of my hands, dear.
Out of my wish to strike the knife
or not to strike,
as if the gods allowed me grace of time
and then struck straight through my will,
and I was no longer free to choose.

The deed was done.

Death of Mohandas Gandhi

Yellow Springs, 1948

Once more the assassin's hand has reached above the crowd
to strike his harsh account for the hidden mutilations
of his heart; and the thin white candle
with the trembling but ever-faithful flame
has blown heavenward, and all the white-robed throngs
cry out "Mahatma, Mahatma!"
But they may bow themselves to touch the ground,
may pray for forty-seven evenings,
may fast to touch the hand of death
(though they dare not, lacking the faith and the will,
else why would they have needed him
to fast the penance for them?).
And the River Ganges may turn back its course
and yield the sacred ashes,
yet no miracle, no act, no sorrow, no cry,
can return that invincible spirit to the aged bony body,
or the keen mind that looked on selfish struggles after power,
the narrow vision, and the imperialistic reaching out and out
across the sacred boundaries of the person or the land.
He saw it all in his own India, and saw it again and
again in the great and powerful places of the world,
and knew the guilt lay within the heart,
and made a Satygraha of his life to right the universal wrong.
Humility and nonviolence—so alien to a heathen world
that hatred springs where lack of understanding lies,
and the few who read the language turn another, safer way.
So one more fluttering candle has left a darkening world,
and our poor groping ignorant hands
may wonder where the hidden door of morning lies.

65

VII

WYOMING

Wind River Canyon

Casper, 1946

Up and down the land the great winds blow.
Up and down and in and out and 'round and 'round they go.
They pass through little western towns
and kick the tumbleweed through the one wide street,
and make the tin sign over the Elkhorn Cafe go
bang, bang, bang!

Up and down and in and out and 'round and 'round,
into the alleys, the boulevards, the broadways of the land,
the great winds blow, besieging the huddled cities
with fury, lashing newspapers against grey buildings,
chasing the discarded knick-knacks of the day into the gutters,
whipping gleefully at women's skirts, tearing the arranged hair,
nipping at the bare legs of children playing in the park.
Up and down and in and out and 'round and 'round
the great winds blow.

I can tell you where they come from.
There's a big cave up in Wind River Canyon in Wyoming,
and every fall a young stripling wind creeps out,
shakes its legs, slides down the canyon wall,
takes off across the plains,
and blows and blows and blows!

Wyoming Legend

Casper, 1946

i

Wyoming is the place of great endless spaces,
where a mile is a step of the way,
and fifty miles is a trip to the grocery store.
Cities are villages two hundred miles apart,
and villages are crossroads with beautiful wild names,
and the wind blowing through them.

Distance is the long swift drive
as over a mile flicks by each minute,
and still the bend in the road is on the horizon's edge.
It is the smooth sail of the buzzard
circling over the plains;
it is the snow-topped mountain peaks
lying against the breast of the sky.
The breathless extension of thought,
unbelievable, yet real.
Distance is the day's trot on horseback
from ranch end to ranch end.
It is the long trains flattening themselves
against the earth to take up their long race
to the Idaho border.
It is the big, speeding cars of ranchers and oilmen
doing an easy seventy miles-per-hour
for hours without slackening,
and still a speck on the horizon.

Wyoming is the big man's shout,
the long train's shriek,
and the lonely woman's cry.
It is the boundless air, the endless wind;
it is the long haul.

Wyoming is the place of strong men;
it takes strength to buck the wind,
to cover the miles,
to bear the loneliness,
to endure the toil on the ranches year after year.
The tenderfeet come and go.
The Wyoming men stay and build the state and raise beef
for the markets of Kansas City, Denver, and Chicago
to feed the open mouth of the country.

You can see the cowboys in town on a Saturday night,
each looking like any other man after his work is done,
except a little more leathery and tanned
by the wind and the sun;
a little more bow-legged,
as if he should have a saddle under him,
clicking his high-booted heal along the sidewalk,
his high western hat pushed back on his head,
his bravado gesture;
and in his eyes still the dazed look of the man
who spends his life riding across
the broad belly of the plains
staring at a sun too bright, at a horizon too distant,
at a song too beautiful for a simple man
of few words to express or understand,
even in his own soul.

iii

Wyoming!
Sing the name! It was meant for music.
Let it roll from your tongue, each syllable growing
until you hear the air and the plains and the hills
in the word even as the winds
carry it in their everyday speech.

The native Americans knew how to place a name
so that it spoke a song
carrying forward the heart's feeling.
The native Americans called Wyoming theirs,

tribe after tribe spilling their blood on the plains
in endless internecine struggle.
Say their names softly as you pick up the delicate
arrowheads (flint and chert, blush-pink to dusk-gray,
all that remains of the noble past).
Blackfeet, Crow, Sioux, and Ute
(hear the thunder of their charging mounts;
hear the wild and hideous war cry of the painted braves;
tomahawks flashing, the frenzy of the kill).
Bannock, Flathead, Arapahoe, Cheyenne
(see them kneeling by the rivers
after the battle is over, the red blood flowing,
spent horses quivering still).
Madoc, Shoshone, Kiowa . . .
(the plains are lonely now that they are gone).

Scarcely do we remember the red man's legend,
or how Wyoming was once his home, and the plains
his hunting ground and battleground,
not the peaceful grazing lands of white-faced cattle.
We honor the great Washakie, the brave Red Cloud,
giving a parcel of land to the subdued kin;
it was the inevitable and harsh effect of history;
no one to apologize, or to forgive;
no one, we hope, to blame.

iv

Wyoming is the place of the long freight trains
shrieking and screaming across the plains
with the ecstasy of wide open spaces,
flicking giant steaming tails of smoke as they roll
across the plains,
cutting through primigenous mountains,
hauling to market their cargoes of coal,
oil, cattle, and sugarbeets
with ease and iron laughter.

It is the country of the yellow clapboard houses
isolated beside the tracks,
and the section crews rolling up and down,
microscopic against the landscape.

It is the place where the long-drawn whistles
sob in the night and sleepers turn in their beds,
dreaming vaguely of space and distance,
and the wide strange eternity of living.

v

Let us speak of the Wyoming mountains now.
Let us fumble with the inadequacies of speech
and the tongue to do honor to this land's halo and glory.

For the mountains are the concluding chords
of this land's symphony, rising majestically,
violently from the plains to the sky.
They were the finale, conceived in passionate fortissimo,
and its music still sounding beyond atmosphere,
soaring through space.

Have you stood beneath them in the winter season,
feeling the spirit leave the flesh and ascend upward,
upward to attend the glistening, infinite peaks,
and then return, to a body strangely exalted, purified?

Have you seen the softness in granite mountain peaks
where the untouched snow molds line into shadow,
upward where union of land and sky is veiled
by mists and the clouds?
Have you seen Wyoming mountains on a winter morning
with the sun half-hidden eastward, brush-stroked
in pinks and rose, while the mists hover grey,
chiffon-like among their heights?
And as dawn meets the clear thin daylight,
the lines of the mountains grow harsh and concentric,
definite unattended rock, outlined
clear and sharp against high, light-shafted air,
challenging and proud, inaccessible except to the eye
and to the flight of the eagle.
And as the night moves in, quickly,
deeply in the valleys,
slowly, slowly among the peaks, enfolding in dark blues
and purples with a crimson outline,

drawing the majesty of height and the closeness of earth
together for a short space of time.

Wyoming mountains bear names given by men who felt
in their souls the magnificent grandeur of their land.
Names that catch the music and carry it forward singing—
Absaroka, Wind River, Teton, Gros Ventre, Medicine Bow,
and the Summer Range, Big Horn and Tensleep, Heart and Pine;
Sweetwater, Laramie, Medicine Wheel, Centennial, Beartooth,
Deer Creek and Elk; Rattlesnake, Seminoe, Squaw, and Sundance.

vi

Wyoming is the place of lonely tar-paper shacks,
bleak beside the highway;
solid ranch homes settled by the cottonwoods and a stream,
and the winds blowing and endless space flowing
around and between, and eyes following the sultry line
of highway, plain, and distant mountain peak.

Wyoming is the place of sheepwagons
picking their lonely path through sagebrush plains,
and the shaggy dogs circling the rippling close-packed herd,
the herder, long silent to speech,
nodding morosely to the occasional seismic crew
prodding the land with strange instruments.
Wyoming is the tiny towns,
half-hidden by the mountain valleys,
half-lost on the bend of the long-curving road;
the one wide street, the handful of houses,
clustered around a church, a school, a hotel, a store,
and the revellings on the highway.

Wyoming is the home of the beautiful shy animals
that hide in the mountains—the elk, the deer,
the antelope, and moose—and eventually must halt
their wild and poignant flight
to grace stores and bars and gaudy restaurants
with their proud repose and dignity.
It is the place of the big oil fields
that turn a barren basin into a derrick city,

74

and the black petroleum standing in slimy pools
around the drilling rigs;
where engineers send sharp steel fingers
reaching down through ancient sands and shales
to bring black liquid gold gushing into freedom
from the long withheld emotion.

Old Indian haunts and animal feeding grounds become
the Salt Creek, Big Muddy, Elk Basin, Little Buffalo,
and Lost Soldier fields,
Mush Creek, Sand Draw, Pilot Butte, and Poison Spider too.
The Wyoming earth experiences new kinds of battles
upon her well-worn, rugged turf, yielding
to the low rumbling wheels of time, and watching
patiently the tortuous and strange career of man.

Wyoming is the place, it is the place
where the horizon is far wider
than the wandering restless eye,
or the frail imagination.
Wyoming is the big breath of clean dry air
scented with the mountain pine
that ameliorates the thought-encrusted mind.
It is the place where the sky holds the earth
in the curve of its arm.
And this sweet affinity ties man more closely
into the foreverness of time.

Hidden Beauty

Casper, late 1940s

Beauty may be found in places obscure and neglected,
such as the backyards of run-down houses
and even the alleys.
I have seen nobleness and grace
in such a poor and unattended place.
An old stone wall set facing the sun,
crumbling with the weight
of western winters and summers
that passed too quickly to be good.
In the bare beseeching fingers of trees that reach
to a distant sky where a scuttle of clouds
pass moving eastward toward the Great Plains.

There is art, there is grace
on the west side of lean-to's
sloping awkward with age and dampness.
I have seen the face,
heard the mute voices on the bright thin air,
with the day waiting to meet the storm
moving in from the mountains in the north.
I have seen art in obscure places.
I have hurried on with the memory of it sharp,
lovely, and still,
among the day's cluttered impressions
and the long night's disturbed dreaming.

Beneath the Aspens

There is stillness and ease and the autumn's peace
beneath the aspen trees.
The morning sun has warmed the earth whereon I lie.
Long grasses touch my cheek with cool slim fingers,
and the trees above have made a framework for the sky.

I watch the ceaseless gentle trembling
of the heart-shaped leaves,
and the thoughts I think are calm and still
and ordered in a row.
There is no tomorrow, no yesterday, nothing but now,
no faces to meet or sights to see, no place I wish to go.

And then the shattered bits of solitude around me fall
as a distant hum turns into a close and constant roar.
A silver plane cuts through my wide and quiet forest sky
on its swift and secret flight to some far, foreign shore.

And suddenly I want it all again with a strong renewed desire—
the roads and the ports and the cities' throng,
the markets' blaze and blare,
and I'm ready to join the eternal crowds
that go and see and do and be and wander restlessly
here and there.

VIII

FOREIGN PLACES

On the Beach at Al Khobar

Yellow Springs, 1977

On the beach at Al Khobar I watch the tide
crawling on its belly,
slow and sullen, toward the shore.
A tired serpent, palavering:
foam spits softly from its lips.
There is no drama here of surging sea;
the Gulf is old and tired and shallow.
The measurements of earth are linear:
flat sand and shallow sea enfilade
each to their own direction into the tilted sky.

The serpent brought me gifts: a starfish,
a sea-horse, a scallop, a piece of cuttlebark.
Their forms are pure and minuscule.
An Arab boy, silent, stern, observes
as I turn them in my hand, wondering, I suppose,
at my absorption with such minutiae,
weighing my motives, wondering from what tribe I come.

This is our world together, child of Mohammed.
These are our common rudiments
dredged up by the ancient sea.
I only drifted farther westward, lost my tribal scars,
lost my footprints in this sand.

Desert Winds

Saudi Arabia, early 1950s

The stars do not change, 'tho the land
beneath our feet may dissimilar be as the winter's snow,
or rain, and the desert's sand, sun-steeped and warm,
on this December night. I may look up
and bless the star for shining impartially on us all
and know your eyes behold them equally as mine.
Ai-ya! It is good to see this light from heaven's lamps,
and to know withal the world is not so vast,
nor friends so far apart.
Salam, the desert winds are whispering, peace!

Street Scene in Amman

Yellow Springs, 1970s

The bougainvillea creeps on dry pastel paws
along my window.
Since dawn I've heard the dry, clean sound
of stone masons — chip and pound,
chip and pound — shaping pieces of eternity.
(The building and rebuilding of Rabbath-Ammon).
There is the smell of honey on the wind.
The season has changed on the hills of Ran.

A child passes, balancing with insouciance
a basket of flat loaves on his head.
"*Khubz, khubz,*" he wails in broken soprano.
A gate clatters.
The handsome Arab who owns the silver shop
below our *jebel* passes, intent and anxious.
He is the lover of my Swedish friend,
and will pass her house longing to see her at a window.
I know she sits within,
her cool Nordic head bent over her work.
She will listen but will not come.
He passes again and again
before returning to the narrow room
where men squat in the doorway,
discussing border forays and the enemy,
without mentioning the forbidden word.

I think of the hills near Ajlun blue-carpeted with anemone,
where I wandered
looking over the Jordan
toward that place one does not name.

Afternoon in Lahore

Yellow Springs, 1977

How pitifully on the ruined day
the scattered shards from the sepulcher
of my defeated dreams
are strewn like withered petals.
The wind tosses them vagrantly across the garden tell
on nets of light and green and shadow.

We bridge players, blinded by delphinium petals,
toss in our hands claiming nothing.
Yonder the velvet sari of the rose bends by the hedge,
where the gardener's face observes us darkly.

His daughter, the sweeper, appears for her evening chore,
scratching the debris with her whisk of reeds.
Faces stare out of shrouds from the shadows,
my face, bare as a full moon and as pale,
holding no honor count.
Farewell, cheerio, adieu, I say; the gate closes.

I beat sun motes with violence, matchsticks for sword,
invoking phantom gods in panic,
chanting my alien litany,
bewailing my trivial soul.

And then, my crumbled spirit is lifted
with the thin and tremulous chant of evening prayer
from the distant mosque
and the charcoal mists rising from ten thousand suppers,
ten piasters' worth of warmth and cheer.
I deal the cards for solitaire, accepting karma.

Rainy Season in Manila

Manila, 1970s

It rained as if it had always rained,
as if there had never been any other condition,
as if skies should always be low and colorless and grey,
as if the atmosphere had always been full
of globs of moisture earth-bound,
and the earth itself accepted
this continual flow with such a non-resistance,
even with a kind of hunger and thirst that
seemed to her gluttonous in its ability to absorb so much,
and the city lay in a kind of soaked torpor,
the brick of the walls across from her window turned dark
with the continual moisture, the roof tiles
glistening with a kind of crapulent delight in it.

Even the people moved sluggishly and passively
through the slush and mud of the streets,
harbored in their rubber and plastic clothing,
shapeless mounds, more like moles or woodchucks,
plodding from burrow to burrow.

It was repulsive.
There should be some rejection of so much rain,
some motion of negation, some withholding
of one's own inherent quality of hardness
and dryness that came from fire or sun, some resistance—
a fist reaching out of a chimneytop and clenched,
shaking itself threateningly toward the dripping sky.

Hunt on the Gambia

Dakar, 1970s

I am cleaning four ducks;
they are brown birds, soft and light in the hand.
The head droops heavy from the long neck,
relaxed in death.
The feet are folded, neatly hiding the web.

I remember this bird or his many brothers
patterned in the sky.
The long neck reached out, the wild cry
came from this throat that I hold now, still in my hand.
I try to imagine these muscles
flexed and hard and that wild sound in the sky.
The wings beat in slow, flawless motion.

Below lay the river and their green familiar island.
They touched the water, waited;
they rose and V'd against the sky.
Embracing the trionym of water, trees, and air,
they circled, separated, met again, and the flock
chose the island treetops
before the thunder of the hunter's gun
ripped the silence from the green hour.
Time shattered, quivered, came slowly together again
as wings reached the sky.
But these four fell.

I pull the feathers — the brown and white striped,
the tan edged with gold, the dark brown.
They come easily from the flesh, tissue-like,
wrinkled like the soft flesh of old women.
I cut with the knife, inserting my hand
to grasp the machinery of life
and wrench it from the frail cavity.
The blood streams into my sink.
I am weak with its flow.

Yet as I ponder this destroyed life,
I remember the heron diving for the silver fish
that jumped and played in the river sunlight.
I remember the *outarde* that dived for the *alouette*
skimming in beauty along the tops of shrubs.
Life gives to life, takes, gives, and takes to itself again.
May the taking be clean and quick and frugal,
and the giving compliant, holding no fear.

Famine

Dakar, 1970s

How do the waves beat now against the rocks,
the black rocks on the Senegal coast
where once we carelessly threw towels
and dove into the foam?
How do the high waves rise and fall
and fall again, foaming white as they pound
their wall of green Atlantic against the shore?
Does some tall thin form still stand staring seaward,
one arm hanging loosely, holding the bag of clams
gathered when the tide was out,
dreaming, perhaps, of heaving ships and other shores?

Or does he face landward, his ear tuned
to the cries from his village home
borne on the wind from the landlocked desert world,
where people move slowly from place to place,
searching for food, their long bones stretched
against the hungry flesh,
the babes big-bellied, clutching the milkless breasts?
The faces—do they turn where the sea must lie,
hearing in the sleepless night the surf's roar?

Or do they think it is the sound of death
the mind contrives,
honing for the final blow?

87

Prayer Beads

Yellow Springs, late 1980s

How many places around the world I've made my bed,
unpacked my bag, found a marketplace, a language,
found the view and come to terms with it,
hired a gardener and a maid,
learned new dusty, winding streets to wander?

And now those lives of mine demand a reckoning.
I take the prayer beads, smooth yellow beads
from the *suk* in a Saudi town,
and I turn each one round with my fingers,
feeling the mystery of weight and value,
of big and small, of ugly and exquisite.

One bead I turn for the Middle East, where
the light I recall is not light, but illumination
that crept over the *jebels*, the vales of Rabbath-Ammon,
over Jerusalem — light at dawn and at evening,
never caring whether Arab or Jew or Gentile
bathed in its radiance,
light and the call from the minaret breaking our mid-day slumber.
The muezzin drew his script like a knife across my table.
The light turned the stark room apricot light;
the shadows were always there on the other side of the light.
The lack of laughter and the acrid taste of longing,
the satiety of love.

A bead for the Andes and those violent peaks
that breathed fire, the Ecuadorian jungle, the taste of danger,
the lurking fear of loss of my children.
I weigh the dusks in Quito when the sunset
fell back behind volcanic peaks,
and the dark came quickly,
quickly sending us to the warmth of the fireplace.
The agony of unfulfilled friendships,
the feeling that home had slipped off the earth
and slid into the cold Atlantic,
The plaintive music of the Quechua,

the Cochabamba parties that broke up at breakfast time,
the nostalgic sounds of dance all night.

A bead for Africa—it takes a long prayer, a long turning
as I weigh the kiss of the ocean over desert heat,
the beauty of bone over the stain of hunger,
the beauty of women with whom I could not converse,
as we walked the dusty road,
our backs loaded with different burdens.
Dakar meant the green-grey sea
and the ships in the harbor,
the ebony-bone faces I longed to touch,
the palette poured into each sunset.

A bead for Asia—Lahore meant a garden of roses,
the measured tap of the *chowkidar*
to tell me he was there, guarding my door,
the dust-filled Grand Trunk Road,
and the panorama of the city at dawn.

In how many places around this planet
have I lit my candle, pondering the mystery
of why some places pull me with the grip of granite
and others fall into crevices of obscurity?

One becomes layers of different selves
patinated upon each other:
the person you were in Bolivia, Ecuador,
the person you were in Taiwan, Jordan, West Pakistan,
Senegal, Tunisia, Spain, or wherever.
For you were different in all those places.
The place, the people made that new layer of self
grow upon you.

IX

IDENTITY

Identity

Golden, 1943

I strive
to find a great white silence, unchartered, infinite,
inviolate of ways and means;

a stillness of the mind,
bearing sounds only of
the understanding stars,
the sun, and perhaps,
the falling of the rain.

And there, upon that solitary plain, I'd meet someone
I used to know, and who, strangely, bears my name.

Phantasy of the Passing Train

Golden, early 1940s

I stood by the fence to watch as they sped swiftly,
swiftly past.
Clickety-clack, clickety-clack,
a shriek and a long-drawn blast.
I saw the white phantom faces;
I saw the wide staring eyes.
Where are you going, I called aloud,
where are you going and why?

But the lips were mute and no answer came
but the engine's heavy roar,
and the trail of smoke covered over the sun,
until it could be seen no more.

Tonight, I lie in my bed and listen;
tonight I toss in my bed and cry,
for I saw my face, I saw my own face,
as one of the cars rolled by.

Sounds of Bells and Trains

Golden, early 1940s

Sometimes I hear the faint and far-off chime of bells
ringing on the morning air.
I can't be sure it's not the wind; I do not know
whether the sound be really there.

But when the bells are chiming, lonely, lovely to my ear,
I think perhaps it is my soul that's singing,
and it's music that I hear.

Sometimes I hear the faint and far-off cry of trains
shrieking their sad legend through the night.
I can't be sure it's not the wind; I do not know
whether I hear the sound right.

But when the trains are crying, lonely, plaintive to my ear,
I think perhaps it is my soul that's weeping,
and it's sobbing that I hear.

None Are Alone

Golden, 1944

No one is a man or woman unto himself or herself,
but a combination, haphazard and strange, of the people
who have entered his or her life,
or those who brushed by in the dark—
a coat-sleeve touched, a hand at the train,
a glimpse in the crowd.
No man is a new man, one and alone,
but the converging shadows of the whole brotherhood.

Some there have been who with brush and palette
have made great strokes, and the canvas is changed.
But the most of a man are those dear, wistful lost faces
of the hometown people who took the boy and became the man.
And some, hardly people, merely a name passed on the lips
or a face seen through the window, or a tale
told by the fireplace, a gossip, a whisper, a name.
They are those never known, yet closer than brothers;
they are the thousands passed by, but long remembered.

None are individuals—alone, strong, and peculiar—
but are the walking form and breathing substance
of so many brothers, clot upon clot of the shapeless clay.
Recognize them in your mirror in the evening,
and turning into the new morning
forget not this kinship nor the way
that the blood is carried.

Jungle

Whether hunter or hunted I cannot tell;
the balance hangs so lightly on each moment,
that seconds are sundust dancing
in insect swarms above my head.
More dark than light lurks in my jungle;
there is an essence of sunlight,
but like a wine poorly made
it wavers in shade, more murky than clear
as I remember sunlight.
My eyes are accustomed to this compromise;
could I look as a child again,
staring at the miracle of bright?
Accustomed too am I to creatures of this green room,
those that cry like friends, that coil, that crouch,
that lie and wait with ever-voracious appetite
for my unguarded moment.
Yet I am clever, can tell by the way a leaf is turned,
a stalk crushed,
where they lie waiting.
And crafty; I bend away the press
of my own footprint.
Sometimes in the velvet hours, I dare to cross a clearing
and lift my eyes to touch the dark
and find imbedded there, at its grainy end,
bright jewels that wink at me, easing my loneliness;
I pretend it is the sky and they are stars.
But would they penetrate this place,
where only the damned howl and cry?

It is here when the jewels gleam brightest
that pagans hold impious revelry,
howling demonic cries, beating drums formed
from the hides of fellow worshipers.
And I hear the eerie anguished tremor of my own voice
raised with those raucous tongues.
Have I turned demon, jackal, wild dog?

I turn and flee into the comfort of deepest foliage,
until the dance is done, holding my fist against my mouth.

We play a waiting game: the hunter and the hunted.
Life is balanced moment to moment:
time is sundust dancing in insect swarms;
fear, the cries from my own throat;
and revelry, the dance that leads to death.
Hunger is the lunge that one day will miss.

Yet sometimes when I pause, panting, from the eternal chase,
I see in one quick cognitive moment all heaven and hell,
and find between my trembling fingers the weapon supreme,
exquisite, of most fragility — I am a man.

Standing Alone

Amman, 1964

I will throw you all from me.
I will pick you clean, as clear
as my passion alone can scrape your bones.
I will ask nothing to take with me,
but shall go fretting for the rest.

You have not healed me, nor filled me,
nor given me any enduring joy.
You have crumpled under love,
have turned yourself away,
taken death as a surer release.
I will no more wait for you,
look for you at the close of day,
but make my own way
in the dense and populated night.
Perhaps back, yet I think forward,
until after much traveling
I can stand alone without you.

Mask-Making Workshop

Yellow Springs, 1970s

She lies on the protected carpet
as I spread vaseline—pressing, rubbing, stroking,
hunting the tense face muscles
leaping against bone.

Bones, I muse, are given to us.
We do not shape them;
expressions and the muscles beneath
we create with the contortions of time
and the claims of character.

I search the secrets in my partner's face,
trying to identify this stranger,
to touch a base of sisterhood. She is tense
and her muscles murmur
"taut and still" . . . "taut and still."

When I am the subject, lying prone, her hands
seek my own roads deepened with weight of years.
I feel the tentacles of my skin
reach for the probe of the nerves in her fingers,
yearning for communication.

The plaster gauze covers me like soil
thrown lightly over a seed.
I cook at low temperature,
the mask adding layers of skin
closed in, covered, except for a straw
tunneling breath to my lungs.

My face is feeling the weight of the plaster.
My face is giving birth to a sister,
an identical twin. I sink into a netherland,
letting the labor flow through me,
accepting the passive role.

99

Then fingers touch me. Voices
probe my solitude. My twin
is being lifted from me.
Help! The pores of my skin cry out.
You are taking my power and
I must face the world naked again.

The Elements of Verbal Subjugation

Yellow Springs, 1970s

What business does Mister Strunk have telling me
where to put my verb? My verb
like my knee or my blasphemy
will be placed where I please.
Why does Mister E. B. White tell me to comma my clauses
when I always prefer clauses that hang
down to my ankles sometimes even dragging
on the ground. Mister White, just bite
off your own adverb and put statements in positive form.
That's your style. My style is repelled
you might say by a rule; some days
I run on thousands of sentences that scramble
like wild trumpet vine growing
with redundant vigor, sentences composed of noncommitted
and luxurious language, needless yet seductive,
repeated over and over like litanies or rhymes.
Mister Strunk, old patriarch, are you still
creating units out of paragraphs?
When any good gardener in the truck farm of human interchange
knows that sentences loose and uncoordinated are the most
engaging and hilarious company one can entertain,
and even nonrestrictive clauses are hardly ever parenthetic
whether related or not; they are naturally dependent
being of the subjugated class, remembering
their place is after the noun
who is head honcho, male, and probably white.
Right, Mister White?

100

Driving Through Mist

Yellow Springs, 1980s

My car and I grope through the shrouded morning
where treetops float like stems of broccoli
and barns sail in a frosted sea.
I know the turns of the road yet am deceived
by floating curtains and the glint
of sunlight vagrant and inconstant.
A monster truck appears out of nowhere.
My car hugs the roadside crushing daisies
that cry of guilt and innocence.

There is the playing field of my old school
where goal posts ghostly and deserted loom.
The school unmoored has lost its dominance.
Yet I pass groping my way still unlearned,
straining to hear some message
that might have lingered.

My headlights help me not at all.
Perhaps they'll warn another car I'm coming,
speeding blindly on my way as if I knew,
as if I knew past, present, and future of my life
the way to go.
I don't know if the sun will lift the fog in time.

101

Disconnected

Yellow Springs, 1970s

No sooner do I let you go across the airfield
than you are sucked into a needle
and injected into a screaming sky.
I think of the sparrows we watched in the morning:
precise and silent, they dipped and soared,
then left on an uncharted journey.

I drive home numb, disconnected,
carrying the dissimulation of your farewell,
light and alone, like
one of the curled brown leaves
driven by wind across the road.
It was your gift when you left:
"Get out of my shadow," you said,
and let me stand in mine.

The indifferent snow begins
to cover the eagerness of your departure.
I rivet my eyes on the highway,
aware in my lateral vision
of space opening up around my horizon
like a door sliding on tracks.
I sense change too new, too subtle to conceive.

The cold wind on my face as I walk to the house
sears my exposed cheeks,
burns my eyes,
hurts my teeth,
bites my legs.
Feeling, again, I know I exist,
and I stand in the entrance
seeing rooms swept bare,
finding everything was left for me:
space
solitude
self.
I enter reeling with joy.

102

Moribund Spirit

Yellow Springs, 1980s

Remembering the letters I should write,
I write none.
Watching the dust accumulate,
I permit it to lie.
Knowing that I should walk,
I do not move.
My spirit is moribund,
and the hollowness in all my limbs and brain
howls like a tunneling wind.

If I wait, it will pass;
but these are pages of my life
torn out blank, or scribbled
with meaningless markings.

X

FAMILY

The Messenger

Yellow Springs, 1984

Like my finger, perhaps the little being
curled in warm and liquid safety,
a worm of sentient life, our little genius,
all soft and hairy, slippery, sleeping
in its mother's envelope.
Oh, woman, you move about that city,
run and vibrate, dance and work, make love,
my grandchild clinging, I think, precariously,
to your womb's lining.

My waves have reached a foreign shore,
and your hidden womb now bears
my genes forever intertwined,
and we move from friends, in-laws, to family,
and the word related becomes reality.

Epiphany to My Son

Yellow Springs, 1980s

I was bearing you full term; the circle was closing.
I was heavy, anxious, as women get.
Then in-laws I had never seen chose that time to visit,
traveling from one part of the country to another.
They came the day you were to come, my son, my son,
disturbing the rhythm of our conversation.
They came with curious stares and brown paper packages,
hiding bruised psyches and broken dreams.
They came like gypsies with dark potions,
and I drank and retched and willed my labor to begin.

Their spells followed me, encircling the doctor,
for he plunged me to such depths
that I never felt your coming,
never knew the awesome thrust or rejuvenating pain
as you kicked, protesting, into our poor world.
After hours of sleep, I asked for you.
"The babies come at six,"
the white herons stated, and would not bring you.
"But I haven't seen him!"
Helpless rage tore and beat through my abdomen.

You cried when I held you, spurning the breast.
The relatives came with advice in chocolate bundles.
I didn't want to share you
nor to hear them say your name.

The night of your birth I dreamed
that I was on a high plateau,
the sky filled with warm and pulsing light
while fine, honing winds brushed past me.
Yet I felt weighted with sorrow, my son, my son.
In that dream my father walked with me,
promising to take care of you,
to purge you of the sourness of my anger,
to right the spirits that worried within me.
My father promised to do that, but he didn't say when.
He didn't say when.

108

A Little Boy at Evening

Casper, late 1940s

My little boy is sad; he doesn't know just why.
He sits so still upon the chair.
His wide blue eyes look close to tears,
and yet he does not cry.

The day has been a trouble; nothing turned out right.
And grown-ups don't seem to understand
a little fellow well.
Yet by tomorrow he'll laugh again,
for gentle is the night.

Little Stranger

Saudi Arabia, early 1950s

Take happiness, do not be afraid, little child.
Show your happiness. Wear it as a jewel on your features.
Let it shine through you, illuminate the air around you.
Do not hide it, do not keep it sealed within like a shame.
Drink of your joy—nature feels herself fulfilled
in your completeness.
The ugly, the mean, the unholy is denied by your joy.
Love is satisfied. Do not hide your joy, little stranger.
Wear it as a flower or as a star,
as a diamond with a perfect setting.
Happiness known well is your heart's protection
from the wounds of pain, from the lonliness, the hurts,
should they ever come.
I say again, little child, little sunshine,
be happy, be happy!

Cider-Making

Yellow Springs, 1980s

They come to help me make the cider —
my daughter and my son.
The cider is 'mother's project.' She lusts
in the rich bronze broth of apples
that pours down the sides of the tub,
fulgent with foaming energy
streaming out like a gusher
across the floor of the press
to the lip and into the pitcher.

They are right. I lust for the richness and ripeness
of the fruits of the orchard — apples
I mothered from dependent trees.
Now I pick this fruit fallen into wet grass
and pull it from heavy boughs,
dropping it into baskets. I set the stage
for the annual ritual. All is ready,
all is provided. The strong muscles of my children
dance in the mottled sunlight.
Their comradely talk dapples the yard,
turning the crank piling in the apples.
Their legs and arms move in rhythm.
And honeybees, high on sugar,
dive like kamikaze pilots
into the fray of our labor.

My children too are seduced by apple cider
lathered in the sweat of growth and sweetness
here in the moist ripe crown of summer.

A Mother's Pain

Yellow Springs, 1970s

Why can I not bear to see my children in pain?
I want to take it back into myself,
as if it were rightly my own.

You are a man now, you do not complain.
You say you're going for a walk
and come back hours later looking sad and tired.
I carried your pain every hour.
You thought you were carrying it alone.
You are a limb, I the trunk;
my sap flows up and through you.
When you hurt, I bleed
sap warm and thick, and the roots that
tie us both to the deep good place
contract with the pain of the bleeding.
They are strong,
they'll survive; the limb will survive.

Housekeeping

Yellow Springs, 1970s

The duet of our housekeeping fills études;
our voices waft lightly in currents
of minute concerns.
We pick up words, then watch them scatter.
Glances are oblique
above the edges of books and the rims of coffee cups,
and our movements through doorways are buoyed
in amniotic fluid that buffers distress
and the imbalance of our separate persons.

A relationship of such length records
in registers unheard in music;
understood in quantum physics.

Absence

Yellow Springs, 1980s

The walls of the room have extended.
I am unable to function, stumbling in open spaces.
Your absence is a drought; I am unable to swallow.
And the lack of you is a lack of breath.
It is painful to speak with others, and the interior
of my thoughts are cuneiformed
with the language of your being.

I concede reluctantly that in time you will come.
I admit, I know, that you live, you move in another
terrain, where there may be laughter and song.
You may be radiant with happiness;
I do not know.
Yet here it is barren and silent;
the threshold remains in shadows,
and the feast is unannounced.

Blood Bond

Yellow Springs, 1980s

Daughter, water, river, flood,
my life travels in your blood.
Summer, laughter, center, core,
as I diminish you are more.
Mask the dancers, decorate,
St. Martin's at the garden gate.
Strike the rondo, sound the flute,
the strings crescendo, the drums stay mute.
Faster, faster, tend the theme,
all will vanish in the dream.
Daughter, daughter, river, flood,
my life travels in your blood.
Winter, warmth, night's long glow,
my fire rekindles as you grow.

Chariots of Fire

Yellow Springs, December 27, 1990

The snow falls straight down; the arms
of the evergreens receive it as their right.
Theirs, finally come, to be nurtured.

My daughter, visiting for the holidays, walks
through the house, regal as an idol, grave,
going about her business.
There is nothing static or quiescent about her,
yet all her energies are disciplined,
held in the internal faith she has for herself.
They are a quiet rain that falls on me,
and I grow watching her.
We are a team, unharnessed, unyoked,
but traveling in the same direction,
pulling in harmony labor put on us by ternal forces.

My son, the sculptor, comes too, now and then,
from his labors. The chisel, the sander, the marble
waiting for his return. We, too, are directed
by the same chariots of fire.

Conflict at Home

Yellow Springs, 1980s

My daughter cries, "You don't understand,
you don't know how it is!"
I see stark involuntary hatred:
I am not slain, being fortified by singleness of intent,
and wrapped in the armor of dual love
for her and myself.

She says she hates me: her words
fly out like rivets of hot steel,
and well she understands their sharpness.
I hold my testimony of love
for she would not screech with anger,
and I rein the skilled venom at my command
for hateful words and her sweet name
are not programmed together in my mind's computer.

I try to say that someday, later,
she will understand, and her answering laugh
as she slams the door
is intended to be hurtful as a knife.
But I hear in it the wild free witchery of youth
and the iconoclasm that my age deserves.

A Daughter's Departure

Yellow Springs, 1980s

Your departure was like a storm abated.
My temperature dropped.
The rooms are cool and wide and empty,
as neat as those display rooms in store windows.
My footsteps follow me everywhere.
The family pets, shrunk to the size of gerbils,
sleep all the time.
I refill their dishes mournfully, and
listen to the quarrels of birds.
Your piano avoids me, closing the whites of its eyes
and silent melodies
reverberate like drums.
I step lightly into your room
and avoid looking at the unnatural
smoothness of your bed, to stand staring
at your dresser trying to make sense
of the odds and ends you left.
In the open closet, the discarded clothes
are limp with self-loathing, waiting
for your shape to rearrange them.

I am lopsided now, my age overbalances.
Tiredness coils around my bones. I don't want love
that brings bereavement. I'll do without joy,
if it must bring pain.
I'll turn the pages of books
and deal cards and crochet mittens.

Return, my love, if only
to walk through these rooms again.

XI

SUMMER

A Straight Road to Plain City

Yellow Springs, early 1980s

It's a straight road to Plain City in the morning.
The grid of fields is shining
and pegged with tiger lilies.
Mondrian cows malinger in one quadrangle,
and the white barns are luminous as castles.
A tall woman in pastel garments
curves like a plunked horseshoe
to the loam of her garden.
My car is the only movement on the landscape,
except for the roadside grasses
snapping their white stomachs as I pass.

Stubborn in Summer

Yellow Springs, 1970s

I'll stay in the air-conditioned room
with the door closed against the voices of the house
and my windows shutting out the conversations
in the garden and the trees.
I don't want to feel the moist green breath
of growth breathing on my neck.
I'll preserve myself like a prune
that has already
taken all the sun
it can hold
and hidden it in a hard tight seed inside.

119

Summer Storm

Yellow Springs, 1970s

The thunder of the summer storm peals and crashes,
breaks and roars.
Yet it equals not the thunder of the soul,
whose roar is muted deep within, and whose pain
cannot such freedom find as the limitless spaces
of the sky.
It beats and clamors, breaks and swells with elemental agony,
and the lightning flashes — blinding, bright-like,
resonating pain.
Oh, come again the dimness and the dark!
Oh, come the torrent of merciful, sweet rain!

Peeping Tom

Yellow Springs, 1970s

We have a peeping Tom in our neighborhood;
he has been seen but never caught.
Standing on tiptoe,
he peers in our lighted windows
looking for real-life drama—
a girl undressing,
a flash of thigh or breast,
someone scratching their butt,
a pimple squeezer at the bathroom mirror,
a father thrashing his child, the outrage
of that face, perhaps, reminding him
of his own distant and entombed pain.
How many backyards does he cross
to find what he is looking for?

Then fleeing from the sudden sweep of lights
turning in a drive, he scuttles
through dark streets toward home
carrying sad erotica: muddy shoes, torn jacket,
stiff neck, and the portfolio of pictures
gathered like ripe fruit from our orchards
riding in his mind. I suppose
he throws himself upon a troubled bed
and plays his own late-night X-rated video
accompanied by a cup of hot chocolate.

Doesn't he know, doesn't he remember
that such plunder will not be bound?
But will return to whom it belongs,
that he's doomed to repetitious journeys
carrying away
only husks
and disconnected cuticles
and scabs of life
which, in context,

become our power,
but carried away
become his hopelessness
his despair?

Noise Pollution

Yellow Springs, 1980s

Tonight a party radios its message,
larking across the lawns.
I lie in my bed listening
until the hours move back to back
across the calendar of sleep.
When I awake, the voices are still there
on the midnight antennae, nay, the early dawn;
light, conversational, continuous
as if the waterfall of normal life
has gone clear mad and forgot directions.

Children are playing in starlight,
their careless voices calling back and forth,
back and forth. Why are they not in bed?
They blather and babble on
while I thrash about, interrupted in dreams,
envious and amazed.

I examine the clock again.
Should I accept their version of the hour?
Should I get up and find my shoes?

But no, they've had enough. Now I can hear
the children bumbling down the road, parents, too,
their voices trailing like tulle and lace
lightly behind them.
A car starts, the soft air blankets the sound;
its lights sweep across my lawn, then plow
a path through the street's dark to the highway.

Now I can turn to my pillow;
no longer do I feel excluded; and find instead
that I listen for the rippling voices
that flowed like a silver stream in the night,
carrying me with them, the uninvited guest.

Repose of the Night

Yellow Springs, 1970s

Without, the summer night is calm and still,
except for the monotone of cricket call
and the soft, light whispering of leaves brushed
by a stray wind running through the dark.

The night is vibrant and alive with happiness,
glad to be free of the harried day,
the din of people moving restlessly,
the roar, the smoke, the blaze and tempest
of wild human life.

The streets are empty, and the skies are still.
Beneath the trees, no one walks.
The rivers are unbroken.
The lake, left to renew itself;
the grass, to grow upright again;
the leaves, to bend and sigh in intimacy and peace.

I touch the cool air so quietly,
hoping to steal the magic of repose
that night has found.

124

XII

GARDEN

Separation

Yellow Springs, 1980s

Take it out! If there be blight,
rip all my garden out!
Let there be barren land where bloom has grown,
let there be void and purity!
It does not cause me pain.
The beans have popped the pod and rolled away,
safe in the heyday of my blooming years.
I'll fallow be. Nay, empty; the garden gone forever.
No tears for unborn harvests.
No wails for the dance of the tasselled corn.
I'll winnow now the grain
and bank the loam against the cold
and never, no, never a thought shall turn again
and never a roving eye
to the ploughman who comes in season
nor the tillers passing by.

Garden Vine

Casper, late 1940s

The vine on the garden fence increases every year.
It pours its multiplying strength
on the garden and the lawn,
unheeded,
unencouraged.
Its leaves are slender polished flutes;
its bitter fruit, although rejected,
keeps offering itself each season,
unashamed.

Butterflies pause on the garden vine
to brush their wings,
and hunted birds find refuge
beneath its tangled growth.

I would like to learn the poise
and grace of such a thing
that has learned to live so calmly,
growing in the season for growth,
yielding in the harvest,
resting in the time of sleep.

Trace Elements

Yellow Springs, 1980s

Junglegreen are my walls, mildewed my ceiling,
Ohiogreen covers the floor, hangs at the windows;
the grey roof leaks acid rain;
even so, there are birds living with me,
singing their scales, clucking and cooing
without stops or rests or other handicaps of time.

The soil is good organic loam;
chemical seepage has not surfaced
and I'll do no more to help it;
rather, I'll harvest buggy fruit and flick away
the tomato worms and transport
limp caterpillars mouthed with cabbage leaves.

Ohiogreen is my home; I lie in its deep night
hearing the corn grow, the shaping of potatoes,
and the somnolent grunts of fat Ohio sows.
Ohiodirt is under my fingernails,
spines from my feet grow down to join
generations of roots in this pasture.

My hair is caught in the twigs of apple trees
I planted, and my lungs hold the dust
and pollens of this steaming canopy.
My skin cracks in the sun and my eyes consume
fire that pours into newly created rivers.
My flesh holds trace elements
of forty local sediments, and I scream
to feel the spike that hafts me to this soil.
Grafted, hybridized, and pruned
this midwest jungle claims me;
the relationships of growth defy the truth,
wherein our minds are honed and tuned.

As the Stalk Withered

Golden, 1944

I slept, and the day drifted quietly past me.
I slept while the yellow leaves fluttered gently to earth.
The asters bent their heads to touch the dry soil,
the stalk withered.
A light wind swept the last husks of summer from the
garden, and on the shed roof a red bird gave a farewell
shake of his feathers; was gone.
Sleeping, I felt these things, and awoke in late afternoon,
saddened as from a dream.

XIII

FRIENDSHIP

Rain

Yellow Springs, 1970s

Rain reminds me of him.
I don't know why—we didn't meet
in a downpour;
never ran
splashing through pools
skyscaped on the sidewalks.
We never met to kiss
beneath an umbrella
in the rain.
Yet rain reminds me of him:
spring rain
or summer, either one.
The feeling of him comes floating back.
Was it a tune we danced to?
"I Get the Blues"?
Or who knows, perhaps I saw his face
flash past in a car as I stood
waiting for someone else
in the rain,
and I caught the tender,
compassionate look
that is him,
and I thought: Isn't everything perfect
in the rain?
And I never forgot the moment.
Perhaps that was it.

Unbroken Filly

Yellow Springs, 1980s

Young filly racing in the clean wind,
red mane tossing, completely erect.
Young filly racing across the wide pastures,
frisking in laughter, stomping in pride,
cutting the turf as you wheel and turn,
snorting impatience, defying all halter,
never at bay.

Young filly racing across the wide plains,
breaking all winds, bucking all storms,
spirits unshattered, bright as the dawn.
Living with ardor, loving with passion,
holding all close, heart deep and tender.
Yet giving with splendor, unflinchingly ever.

There is a word for you.
There is a poem for you.
There is a throat-ache, a heart sob,
a song singing on the lips for you.
Beautiful filly, child of the free range,
to the clean, open winds of the land you belong.

Mislaid Jewel

Yellow Springs, 1980s

We met again after so many years
we didn't want them counted.
We faced each other fiercely, bruising.
The bantering words masked
the exploring eye of the hidden camera
recording the slaughter of the years.
I felt the probe of your thoughts
stirring around in the hieroglyphics
of our conversation,
seeking to discover
who or what I had become,
to balance your stored image
of what and who I was then,
and all my tentacles thrashed
through the space between us
trying to touch the fabric of your life,
judging its texture, color, and worth.
And afterward, all the messages
I had gathered
blended into one kernel of feeling
belying time, knowledge, judgment,
saying only some jewel
of undetermined value had been mislaid.

Sisterhood

Yellow Springs, 1980s

I hated to say good-bye.
Time, like a desert flood,
will erode between us before we meet again.
I have made a mental monument in the emptiness you left;
it reads: a friend, who never intruded
into areas of criticism or judgment;
she was loving and still,
a continuer and a companion.
I felt your acceptance of me and my choices;
you would not compare, define, or limit me.
I felt a free person in your presence.
You have taken steps toward your freedom,
and I envy you.
My way goes in a different direction,
its progress obscure, minute; I am still unraveling
the skeins around my ankles so I may move forward.
Watching, you were patient.
You did not say, "Why?"
and you did not lead or coax me to move faster.

We are sister-daughters of Mother Earth.
More correctly, we are sister Earthmothers,
facing old age,
trying not to look at death steadily,
trying not to look back too often,
trying to watch what our hands are doing,
to read the words on the page, to follow
the heart's instructions carefully,
feeling it important that we miss nothing
that will add to the completing of our person,
and that nothing intercepts the messages
arriving constantly.

Without each other, our vision is limited.
Send me your gleanings; I shall send mine.
The world is not always kind or beautiful or helpful.

We must remember how it was
in your kitchen,
drinking tea,
the circle of warmth.

Airwaves of Memory

Yellow Springs, 1980s

This has been a stone-hard winter.
An invading enemy conquered a strong woman,
leaving her helpless as this nuclear war
of the cells defeated all resistance.
Tears and anger, guilt and fear and envy
all stirred into the porridge of our grief,
so even the forsythia closed its eyes.
April is more than cruel this year.

Judith Rose Gray Winnick — reluctantly
our pens draw a line through this name
on our lists of social justice activists.
But the cancellation of that name will not
obliterate the sight of that smile,
the sound of bubbling laughter or righteous anger
hanging still on the airwaves of memory.

Driven Woman

Yellow Springs, 1980s

I put the fire in because she's coming;
she's drifting in to see me
midst a rare winter blizzard in Ohio.
She's drifting in behind the wheel
of a front-wheel drive Japanese car.
This woman, propelled by high-octane natural energy,
has driven in high gear from the age of sixteen,
creating feats that would catapult most women
(and all men) into driveling idiots,
nursing nature's misdeeds (and we learn how misdeeds
can be lovable as hell coming as they do
out of our own innocent
and amateur attempts to improve the human race),
nursing, as well, some of nature's most delightful
creations, earning degrees,
joining the military to feed her kids,
working twenty hours a day.
Now she's drifting in from the country
to see me, to network,
to confirm our friendship
and reconfirm it again and again.

Dinner Party

Yellow Springs, 1980s

The drinks are more cautiously taken;
the h'or d'oeuvres are healthy.
We laugh a lot, at ourselves mostly
and gently at each other,
remembering the wild old times,
gossip of secret encounters,
of success at tennis, pregnancies,
and dress-up balls, the years
the children went to college.

We order fish for dinner,
omit potatoes, dessert;
we are careful, you see,
protecting the time that is left
to be together, to play
a couple of rubbers, to have two drinks,
to watch the birds,
and go out for dinner.

XIV

PROTEST

Ideal World

Yellow Springs, 1970s

If I did not live in a world poised on the edge of
disaster,
    I would spend a month in spring planting
    seedlings of trees that are available free;
    I would crusade against littering, sorting beer cans
    from trilliums in the countryside;
    I would climb a mountain, passing through
    valleys and villages with happy, curious people
    and climbing above their terraces of grain;
    or perhaps sail a leisurely boat to an island
    to read philosophy.

If I did not live in a world that spends all its wealth
on bombs and submarines of death,
    I would organize art shows and concerts free for all;
    and we would have money to buy books and sculptures
    and make parks full of flowers and trees and cascading
    fountains; and there would be playing fields
    and tennis courts open to anyone.

If I did not live in a world where silos
are made to hold missiles,
    everyone who wanted could work — the women,
    the minorities, the youth, and the men.
    There would be day-care centers, libraries everywhere,
    markets for artisans and farmers.
    Government would patronize the arts and fund research.
    There would be no weapons to buy, no armies to pay.
    Our children would give birth to children
    instead of restraining their parenthood,
    and we would be grandparents encircled with love and peace
    in a world whose potential stretched over us like a rainbow.

If I did not live in a world that daily prepares for war.

The Birthright Custodians

Yellow Springs, 1980s

Hey, officer, put down your bullhorn!
Don't order me about!
Listen to a woman's voice! Listen to what I have to say!

Our ancestors for generations have spread their sweat
and spit and blood and finally their whole shebang
of skin and bones nourishing this soil.
They built, cultivated, birthed.
They kept the vestal fires alight, the water pumping,
the crops growing, the factories turning out goods
that all of us consume.
They tried to make democracy work and education a birthright
and jobs for everyone and the White House an abode of honor.
So they failed, but we the inheritors don't default.
It's still ours to rejuvenate, to remodel, to create again.

We were promised we could live free on this land,
not burned to a radioactive cinder by the bombs
that your bombs have been creating from the enemy
that you created out of synthetic whole cloth.

You are turning our heritage into pastures of death,
plotting the craters you'll create in the cities over there.
Your chain-link fences and barbed wire guard cargo
with coded bills of lading that no longer are a secret.
Your closed gates we shake with our sobs
open to trucks that pass like giant earthworms in the night
loaded with cankerous disease, with infamy,
with cargo our ancestors would have sworn no mortal man would
dare to create in the face of his God.

When we criticize, officer of the U.S. Army, listen!
When we protest, don't confront us with your puppet MPs!
When we demonstrate, don't put our mugshots in your files!
Take our fingerprints, send us up for stepping
over a yellow line you had painted this afternoon!

We are the birthright custodians of this land!

144

First Strike

Yellow Springs, 1980s

Do not tell me that first strike, or first use,
is something to consider! There is no choice
between ultimate evil and ultimate annihilation.
Could we continue living a good life if a hundred
million Russians were incinerated in a first strike?
Could we eat and sleep well with the Russians obliterated?
Would our children grow up healthy,
feeling just splendid that here in America
we could play baseball, go to movies, shop at the mall?
Would the president, sitting in the Oval Office,
say "Damn, I hated to do it,
but now let's get on with something else."

Soft Targets

Yellow Springs, 1991-92

They talk of night warfare, stating 'We own the night,'
as if the words make it so.
I think the other side believes
the stars are theirs, too, yet I will not quarrel
with which army owns the night.
We women know it is not ours.
Yet when they speak of missiles
and classify them as effective on soft targets,
it is no secret what those targets are.
I do not know the sound they make as
they splay into soft and pliable skin,
dive into the warm heft of blood vessels and
brain sacs, crush the hot river of the guts,
but I know that the children of women
of every race are wasted on sea and sand,
and fall through innocent skies,
and it matters not when night descends who owns it.
The buzzards feast in daylight.

The Data Collector

Yellow Springs, 1980s

My work is with the Department of Sanitation,
International Division. Collect data, I was told,
remain calm, impartial, dispassionate.
Sunday is free, you are released from duty, have fun
(they do not know how I spend my Sunday).

On Monday I'm at the wheel, a new litter bag
for the weekly collections. Perhaps, I pretend,
in the bright Monday light, it will not be needed;
yet my collection begins. Torture in El Salvador
and the Philippines; in Florida an execution.
As I swerve into Tuesday, a child is raped, a woman
dies from a beating, an earthquake in Turkey.
Wednesday totters with its load of ill: on Maple Street
a man dies for lack of affection and a young woman
hangs herself in jail. I think of the forgotten person
sitting in solitude year after iron year.

My bag is heavy on Thursday as I drive through
the streets of Bhopal, and my hands sweat as I turn
into Friday to find famine in Tanzania and a friend
with her gut riddled with cancer. The statistics
of acid rain spell the pH of ruin.

Oh, Saturday's child will never grow
to be Sunday's parent or the bearer
of Monday's burden. My bag is outside
filled to the brim; I hear it explode
with its putrid load
as I sit in my house on Sunday,
my free Sunday,
and I cry and I cry
and I cry on Sunday.

147

Ululating

Yellow Springs, 1980s

As I kneel on the dry ground,
the spiders flee to give me room;
the bird in the tree leaves instantly;
the dry leaves speak beneath my legs.
I tell all frightened birds,
insects and unseen spirits
to be undisturbed.
I have come only to mourn,
to utter prayers and ululate.
I command my cat who followed
to keep her distance.
I want this space;
it is mine to rend;
I must have room;
I must have space to mourn.

I lift my hands with aromatic ashes
and let them fall
over my hair and shoulders;
my lips catch the lovely acrid taste
of autumn.
I smell long winter fires;
my weeping flows.

Ulululululu . . . who can speak grief?
Who can write pain?
I mourn for my great grandchildren,
mourn never-to-be-born babies;
I mourn helpless mutated creatures,
mourn for this planet and for history.
I weep for leaves and spiders and cats and children,
for the harmony of seasons, the generational urge,
the patterns of birth and age and dying.
I mourn for clean water, for fruit,
for letters from friends, the meeting of friends,
even departures, the whistle of trains.
I mourn dreams of journeys we will not take

into the star-filled universe,
the unnatural, the dead, stillness.

I mourn the flaw in my race
that could not prevent this,
and I weep for God, for theology
that lied and silenced
and never intervened.

XV

AUTUMN

Season of the Poets

The summer closes, and the days come frost-tipped,
yet warm and mellow at the core.
I can hear the golden murmur of the harvest rise and fall.
Why do the purple shadows in my garden deepen more and more?

It is the season of the strange and urgent longing,
the time when the heart is wild and sad,
and the bones crack and strain with their desire.
The time when the fast trains send back long cries in the night
and we listen in our quiet beds, touched with the
melancholy we do not understand,
reaching out for the one,
the something that is not there,
hearing the step in the street outside,
and the dry leaves rustling.

It is the season of the poets: of Tom Wolf whose strong goat-cry
reechoes in the North Carolina hills;
of Robert Frost, pausing in his New England garden
to watch the wind swaying the birches;
of McLeish and his Conquistadors,
thundering through a nostalgic past;
of Sandburg in the golden harvest of his wheatfields;
of Masters among the dry grasses of the Spoon River graveyard;
of Jeffers on his lonely Pacific shore;
of Aiken straining the dry earth through his fingers.
To all of the poets now and before, the autumn belongs.
I, in my doorway, listening,
hear above the cacophony of the street
the resounding poetry and song of the season,
hear the symphonic reverberations of the ripening land,
hear the calling, the pleading, and never the answer.
Oh, why must the brown leaf crumble, crumble in my hand?

Autumn Sonata

Yellow Springs, 1970s

Seedpods hanging like streamers in the catalpa tree.
Tassels of goldenrod brushing the pebbled road.
Veils of mist violet across weeping forests.
And jewels in wanton disarray, dropping like rain.
The highbush cranberry
hangs like Iranian tears,
and the common birds
sway on the wire,
pondering the motion of air
and the range of their wintering.
The hours, I think, slither by
like beads in the telling.
I am a harp and on my breast
these autumn minions
pluck and strum their repetitious airs,
and I tremble in the pellucid rain
of their ancient music.

Old October

Casper, 1945

Footfall and crackling leaf, the cool and brittle silence.
This is October; this is the month (yes, this is the time) when
the silent heart cries out for earth's ecstasy . . . is over.
(There is still warmth on the ground among the brown grasses.)

This is the long month—the trumpeter sounding his dawn-cry over
forsaken marshes, the voice
calling in the night's stillness
remaining unanswered.
(Footsteps pass slowly down the long street,
shuffling the dry leaves; a door closes.)

Oh, brown and acrid month, month of remembering,
turn your golden noon around and turn your amber
twilight southward.
Hold back the red leaf falling, and the brown nut
twisting on the bough.
Join not the resolute geese in flight to eternal summer.
Turn home, turn home! (Yet where is home? Is it gone forever?)
The trains call out;
their naked cries fade into dark, unending distance.
October—this is the time to let the heart bend backward,
the month to be alone.

Season's End

Casper, late 1940s

Late October has come again,
that wistful time of the year,
when some of the hours are mellow and warm
and some are cold and drear.
The swift, strong winds have come again,
tearing the bright leaves down.
The streets are glutted with golden shreds
and a sadness haunts the town.
Autumn was here with the colors, the cheers,
the gay brassy band,
but it rounded the corner and left me
with a crumpled balloon in my hand.

Autumn was here, I remember the day,
and the passionate words that were said,
remember the hour when the whole earth blazed
and the frost-crumpled vine was red.
But now comes the fury, the torment,
the madness of wind and storm,
and the land stands brown and bruised like a bird
when its feathers are shorn.
I shall find me a doorway to crouch in, and hide in, and cry,
because autumn once more has been here and touched me,
and once more passed me by.

October Woman

Casper, 1945

October is scurrying down the street,
scuttling her brown and twisted feet,
tearing the shreds of her faded red hair,
with tatters a-flying in the gusty air.
Stumbling, she passes, not a moment too soon,
here choppy dum diddle comes November's tune.

November Forenoon

Casper, late 1940s

The morning sunlight streams into the street,
bringing old patches of snow into new loveliness.
Bare branches sway slightly in an unseen breeze,
and an old cat walks from a back door alongside
the house, her tail caressing the clapboards.
Across the street, through a kitchen window,
a housewife wipes her breakfast cups and saucers,
twirling her towel in each one with deft movements,
stacking them before her neatly, while her glance
rests dreamily on the sunlit street below.
Sparrows, like good children, play quietly in the gutter,
and an old man passes on his way to market.
Down the main avenue, a car speeds; and up above
drones the distant flight of army planes.
But on this street, there is the even certitude of
morning.

Weeping Forest

Golden, early 1940s

The forest, wounded by the wind,
weeps dead leaves.
The dark lurks behind denuded shrubs.
My uneasy steps hesitate on the path.

Why so wintry, friend?
Summers are also our fate, and glorious autumn.
Brush the leaves from your face and garments.
The trees whisper lessons.
The sustained musical note of the quiet woods
is a message of recovery.
Succumb with me to this seduction.

The shape of a leaf is divine.
Even this small recognition connects us to God.
Taking the life of an ant or a worm
builds scar tissue layer upon layer over misdeeds
and weights us toward earth, not heaven.

Wind in Autumn

Casper, late 1940s

The wind is a mad woman,
shrieking,
tearing her hair,
running with awkward, unbalanced strides,
as her demons dance
and
howl
in the
air.

158

XVI

NOCTURNES

November Night

Yellow Springs, 1970s

Outside, the night was remote and cold; the moon,
a thin crescent, was hid again and again by the restless clouds.
A neighborhood dog barked, business-like and unexcited;
was still again.
Through the silence drifted a thin threat of
conversation, unintelligible, elusive,
and then died away like steps going down the street.
The coolness of the November night crept into my still room,
surrounded my bed.
I thought persistently of an old friend, wondering where,
in what city,
in what room, she was now, what she was doing.
Troubled by this little thought, I fell asleep in the
impersonal arms of the night, as the neighbor's dog
began barking again.
The clouds drifted over the moon.

Waiting Alone at Night

Casper, late 1940s

The depth of the night is never known,
except to those who wait alone
on to the dark hours through
its long dark alley that leads into morn.
To traverse it, one must become each night reborn.

Fear is a soul mate, yet not of the dark or the terror.
But for the key that may not turn, the step not heard,
the door not firmly shut, as is his way.
Fear is that the waiting may be too long,
that the taut heartstring may tremble, shimmer, break,
or the void of sleep might blot away the terrible majesty
of his return, denying the heart its meek, small triumph.

Fear holds one hand, and hope the other,
and the hours push headlong tumbling into morn,
where the gentle hands of sleep at last push down
the eyelids and hold firm.

Nocturnal Meeting

Casper, late 1940s

The trees do not hide the moon, though they try.
Their dark hands gesture wildly and spatulate against the sky.
Yet my eyes meet the eye of the night and are entranced,
and my soul lies naked at last.
The searing of that glance
is a pain that holds a strange and awful agony.

I am known. I am not alone.
Now I walk through the night with this kinship joyful
within me.

162

Night Walk

Yellow Springs, 1982

In the darkness, I walk through my house.
There is no light anywhere; at the end of the room
the windows are soft grey mouths.
My antennae hands brush walls and furniture
that sit in their places unmoving like friends,
allowing me the freedom to use them
in my exploration. At the head of the stairs,
I stand by a pit of darkness,
lost in the immensity of non-seeing,
content not to speak, not to see, to be alone.

Seeing nothing, I feel disembodied, ethereal
in the blackness, and I wonder
if I have ceased to be; but then
a current, a synapse, races through me,
connecting me to the universe.
I am not lost, not dead, not forgotten.
Exultant, I want to remain
here in the black beloved night,
where I can believe in my self,
in my self irreducible by light or voices or the world of men,
just the incredible spark that is my life
and know no other needs at all.

Song of the Night

Who is this God omnipotent whom we have named the night?
Appear, oh, you, who rule between the dusk and dawn!
Have you a heart, a soul, a mind that moves?
Does your darkness hold deep hidden thoughts,
or drowse away in dull indifferent duty?
Speak, oh voice of the night, for I am mankind,
and I demand a knowledge of your mystery.

"Oh, little mankind, who clamors for my secret,
oh, mortal one, who trembles lest there yet exist
a master you have not subdued or snared
into the museum of your colossal conquests!
Then listen, I am not afraid nor am I envious,
nor have I a mystery to hide from your microscope.
I will reveal my heart, my mind, my soul to you.

Philosophers, astrologers, scholars, and scientists,
lay aside your emblems, your symbols, and measurements
and listen to the lay of a poet, the song of the night.
For the mother who at sundown leads her children
into the nursery to their waiting beds,
who sings a soft lullaby and tucks in the blankets,
who leaves a caress and closes the door.
It is she who knows my secret; she is my soul.

And the beating you hear in trembling and wonder
and think is the heart of my deep, hidden meaning
is humanity's heart, the heart of all people,
that you hear in the hours your machines are still.
It is the hot heavy beat of the midnight lovers;
it is the rhythmical beat of the sleeping children;
it is the delicate beat of the dreaming aged;
it is the toneless beat of tired workingmen.
I have no heartbeat but a symphony of people.

And my mind that you fear lest it see too keenly
into the sly secrets that belong to mankind,

this also I return to you kindly, for I am a poet.
The mind of the night is a lonely seeking thing.
It exults, it triumphs, it is baffled,
and beats against bars.
It dwells in the study; it sweats in the lab;
it slinks in the alley; it cries in crowded taverns;
it paces deserted streets.
The mind of the night is a ubiquitous, noble thing.

I am the voice of the night and I am receding again.
I shall become a whisper, a sigh, a current of air.
And you shall forget that I have ever spoken,
for my mystery was no illumination, I am no prophet.
I am only the daylight that at evening smiles,
sighs, turns its face to the wall and falls
gently asleep.
I am her closed eyelids; I am her sleep; I am the night."

XVII

TIME

Corridors of Time

Yellow Springs, 1980s

Awakening, I condemn my clock
as if its voice had summoned me,
instead of my own timepiece deep in cerebral folds.
I grope toward retreating dreams,
swimming into depths that are part of me, yet not mine.
An integral was there that energized my faint spirit
with the current of tumbling dreams.
I do not know how to name it.
Was it hours or centuries that moved in long horizontal rows
across continents of the mind?
Like the ocean's tide, moon and sun undulating,
like winter's white and summer's green accelerated
on the screen, those moving sentinels of time pressed on me.
I was involved as oxygen is involved in
breathing, as the moon in tides.
Yet now I am thrust away,
a child pushed into the schoolroom,
left to its tenuous powers.
Sometimes my panicked cries escape;
sometimes joy streaks like a spring wind from my throat.

Which is the real dimension? Was it there
in the orifice of the dream under the despotism of sleep?
Or is it here in the corridors of time — where the clock
ticks in ill-formed ethnic language,
and I with sensation's ancient plow must stumble
through scheduled hours, my rehearsal for the role that waits
again in the wings of sleep?

169

Entropy of Me

Yellow Springs, 1980s

Time has flattened, become an elongated plain.
In my made-in-Japan car, I grope for maps.
I have no sense of direction; everything
accelerates, even the entropy of me;
There are so few turns.
No longer the landmarks of children's births,
of loves coming and leaving;
no end of school to work for;
no beginning when the children
depart and give me room to breath.
Rooms have no walls now.
The months roll into each other unpunctuated.
My daughter, late born,
forms the boundary of this plateau,
keeping me from falling off,
soaring into stillness.
Yet my wheels spin in protest. There is still power,
but, somebody, please, give me a sign!
Decipher the roadsigns! Translate the maps!

Chords of Fate

Yellow Springs, 1980s

The clock stopped some time before I came. She said
the key was too hard to turn.
Knobby and weak, her hands smooth the polished arm
of her chair . . . there . . . it is wound.
As I turn the clock hands, the half-hour
touches the air lightly.
I turn and the clock strikes ten;
resonant notes fall into the room
like meteors striking the earth
dropped from a granite source
into the room . . . where the rocking chair
moves ever so slowly with the listener
who waits . . . who waits for time.

I turn the hands to find the Now.
Again and again, the hours strike as we listen,
having their say . . . their hour heard and fully noted
in this room . . . in her room.

Moving these symbols of time I tremble,
playing God with my mother's time,
with the last hours of her life . . . the precious
stock of time . . . none to be lost
none to be sold or traded.
Or is it my own life I tremble for
in these ardent chords of fate?
I stand at the clock . . . she sits . . . and we wait
for all the round full drops of life's elixir
to fall . . . one by one . . . into her lap,
into my bloodstream.

Rainy Day

Yellow Springs, 1970s

The rain drums endlessly on my window.
The room is long and thin;
the afternoon without juice, and voiceless;
the hours on the clock shapeless bundles
of minutes, holding no meaning.

Oh, for the midnight hour on the highway
with the wind blowing
and the pandemonium of life reeling around me!

Inner and Outer Time

Golden, early 1940s

Inner time is limitless — from past lives
I can no longer remember, only feel.
Time flows,
and around me a continuum
moves and swirls, engulfing me,
and moves majestically beyond
my inner sight or imagination.
This time is immense, a celestial sphere.
Yet it does not forget me, does not neglect me.
It embraces me. I am a part of its verity.
It is part of mine.
My life flows, it flows.

Our Moment in Time

Casper, March 1946

And in the immense and ravaged wastes of time,
in the long slow evening of the world,
where will this moment be?
This one sure moment held against all emptiness
and doubt, this certainty, this hunger fed,
and thirst fulfilled?
Will its grave history not be kept
in the volume of eternity?

And then the night moves in,
and when the restless sea begins its thunderous wash
upon the desolate shore, and the earth is taut with stillness
and the sleeping death, will not there somewhere
hang our story, obscure and simple,
yet profound with happiness?
Will it not even echo in the wind
as the random plucking of an instrument
might linger drifting, troubled, in the air?

Will the earth roll on forever, in the immensity of time,
forever unmindful of this tiny precious hour?

XVIII

WINTER

The Coldest Winter

Casper, late 1940s

It was the coldest winter; icicles threatened
us at our doorways, the snow whined beneath footsteps,
the breath steamed like puddings.
Children were indignant, unschooled in discomfort,
and the elderly, wrapped in their chairs,
snapped and complained.

In the streets, homeless animals moved numbly
away from the traffic, their tortured eyes
had lost contact with hope.
Garbage turns into stone at twenty below;
some kind of shelter is essential.

I passed in warm garments, food awaiting, warmth.
Yet I kept watching those dogs in the street,
sensing a bond, not understanding,
and I thought of them at night in my room
and discovered the reason.
Deprivation is not just of the body.
The plateaus of sisterhood
cross chasms of infinite dimensions.

Frosty Night

Golden, early 1940s

I walk through the frosty night,
the cold, like tiny soldier knives, stinging my face.
The austere moon is cold,
and the stars immobile in the sky.

The world tonight is a great cathedral
with a Bach chorale filling the place
with its cool wide tones.
The stars are the tiny windows up above,
the moon the altarpiece, and on my cheek upturned
the drifting snow lays white soft hands of love.

Etching

Golden, early 1940s

Etchings of the winter evening slowly blending into night
bring a fresh baptism, religious in its splendor.

Deep, soft drifts, and one brown sparrow
hopping dispiritedly from bush to bush.
The clump of cottonwoods a black silk screen;
fenceposts — solitary sentinels knee-deep in snow.
And one homely bush, now delicate, in white suspended.
Even the sky restful, free from color, from light,
descending patiently to meet the drowsy night.

And over all the heavenly strains of a favorite aria
and the warmth, the lamplight, the mellow hour;
the sweet burning thoughts of lover and friend.

Oh God, oh snowstorm, oh etching of evening,
never end, never end!

Illusion in Winter

Golden, 1943

The door closed tight behind me.
My feet made soft imprints across the snow.

Above, the sky hung low and brooding.
The mountains hunched, grey hoods pulled low.

A melancholy silence pressed about me,
until my winter-weary heart cried out in pain.

Then suddenly I heard a movement, vast and stirring.
I heard the swift, retreating patter of myriad tiny feet.
I heard the frozen trees moving in their slumber
and pink-tipped buds stretch forth a trembling hand.

I looked—and there, behold! Where ice and snow had been
a full-bloomed pear tree shimmered in its fragile gown.
And to the left I turned in time to see
a yellow forsythia shake gently, and preen,
and dance a farandole.

My head grew giddy with the sweet, intoxicating scent
of lilacs, honeysuckle, plum,
until reeling I ran, hands outstretched, groping, to
press and hold the graceful pear blossoms—only to know
with my own touch that they were there.

Oh! What is this stuff that's falling
through my fingers?
Alas, poor heart, my hands are holding snow.

Infants of Destiny

Golden, December 27, 1942

The snow lies deep and soft tonight;
the air is sharp, brittle, piercingly sweet and fresh.
The world lies supple in the arms of the old year.
quiescent in the days past, hopeful for days to come.
We pluck thoughtfully at the frayed edges of this year's
petticoat, touched by remembrance of past warmth of
people we loved who passed with us these days.
Yet half ashamed we turn from the year's shabbiness,
longing for the new, the untried, the fresh.
What will the New Year bring? What will we,
tottering infants of destiny,
bring about with these hands,
these finite brains,
these pygmy imaginations,
this match-flame of faith?
Oh, may it be the awakening of spirit in sterile minds!
May it be the maturing of intelligence, latent and cold!
May it be a daring, a courage more powerful than steel!
May it be the answer to the prayer of the ages:
the ever-sought-after, never attained,
all-prevailing, all-embracing
love!

Dream of the Winter Solstice

Yellow Springs, 1992

It is the year's dead-end; the calendar has built its wall.
The bare-blown trees lacerate the sky, and clouds pull down
darkness into the pathways, the corners,
the despairing streets, abbreviating the day,
darkening the dark.

In some parts, they offer candles and music against
the accursed winter and the gathering of silence
to exorcise disease and sin and avoid perhaps
the horror of the abyss.
The winter of our lives is neither sin nor despair nor madness;
the winter holds its own gifts
that the holidays symbolize but do not supersede.

I wait in the alleyway, sheltered from wind,
for my entrance to the equinoctial rite is not yet.
I breath deeply, pushing out pain with life-affirming
breaths of universal energy filtered through the laden and acrid
air of mid-continent industrial.

A small animal darts across my feet seeking refuge,
and I move obligingly.
Perhaps she too prefers to listen to the bells and voices
and the ragged sounds of music in the distance.
Here in the alley dark, I wait.
Perhaps for grace. For knowledge. For trust.
When it comes I will know it and march out proclaiming:
this, then, is my life, its shreds and tatters,
unfinished, yea,
too late learned, underdeveloped like an emerging
republic of hopefuls.
I will speak my lines, smile my official smile, embrace, perform;
but it is, you understand, a learned exercise.
I am still the acolyte, training 'till the end.

Here in the shadows I sense a movement and tense
lest my space be rent with others.

But I am in deep shadow and now I hear the bright hiss
of life-affirming urine, and my mind images
the growth of a puddle behind a bush,
and with the same slight movement
he is gone and silence is again ours.

There is a high note. Swirled overhead.
I listen wondering if it signals the quintet
warming up to perform.
It is twisted around a tin exhaust pipe on the tavern
roof and there resounds.
It is only the teasing wind.

The wind brings, instead of fresh pine or willow,
the urine scent of too many passersby,
who have stepped into this space to pass
life's precious poisons,
unmeasured on this passive earth.

A group of children pass, and instinctively I send
my child-self forth to join them.
I watch her leap with her gauche freedom
into their midst, never doubting her welcome;
see her rough-cut blond hair, her homemade dress,
her gartered stockings, her worn shoes.
But she moves as if the street is familiar,
and the procession a dance with a part outlined for her.
The world belongs to her, and she to it.
There are no reservations, no doubts.
See her prance, watching the others to mimic, to belong.
She is wild with delight. Innocent of sorrow.

And lights exploded in the sky — violet, crimson, blue,
and there follows a sound so big
instinctively I recoil and hold my ears.
I look to the sky again expecting bonfires there,
but see instead three letters spread from side to side:
JOY   JOY   JOY
and something wild and beautiful and strong grabs me
and flings me into the sky
where I whirl across trees and towers and fields,
feeling only the strong surge of wind

and power caressing my bare face.
We—the wind, the sky, and I—dance a lusty dance,
macabre, and the sound of
JOY   JOY   JOY
reverberates like a drumbeat.
I am back again at my alley post and try to still
the veins that move with low content. . . .
and beat the heart with sluggish joy.
Our body's fetid mentoring of age and soil. . . .

And he who sleeps beneath the oleander bush
may never ever wake again.

The plinth of sound of a small fish
cutting the water's edge and disappearing again.